SEASONED WITH EMPOWERMENT

STORYTELLING FROM THE KITCHEN

SEASONED WITH EMPOWERMENT

Book 1 from the

S.H.E. Aloud movement

Where Stories Heard Empower

Holistic
Storytelling
Publishing
House

Published by Holistic Storytelling Publishing House 2023

Paperback ISBN: 978 1 7395353 08

eBook ISBN: 978 1 7395353 22

www.nixiefoster.com

Holistic
Storytelling
Publishing
House

This book is dedicated to all women whose voices have been silenced.
May we be the key that unlocks the cage and gives power to you and your voice.

Together let's continue to break the bias and be SHE Aloud!

Preface

Most of the women I connect with have been told…

- *Be a good quiet girl* (I was told this so much)
- *You are so dramatic* (This I was told even more – in fact, I still get told it)
- *No one wants to hear it* (And this, I still don't know why my voice matters less than a man's)

This, all of this, has made the voices of women QUIET... SHHHSSSS!

As I began to unlock my voice from the cage that over a decade of domestic violence had placed it in, I began to find my way back to me. The young girl who watched a famine on TV and didn't understand why the big people – the adults weren't doing anything. The teenager who organised petitions and walkouts for human rights. The art student at university who found a new way to stand up for women's rights. And I found nothing had changed from 1999, when I graduated, to 2023. Women's voices were still being silenced, mocked, and disregarded. The same issues, experiences, and injustices were the fabric of everyday life for women and girls. This ignited the fire of my soul and I decided I would do all I could so that no woman's voice was silenced ever again.

And so was born "Seasoned With Empowerment", a book collaboration to begin a movement – S.H.E. Aloud, where Stories Heard Empower. This was never about just a group of women telling their stories; it was about showing how in the everyday ordinariness of a woman's life lies an extraordinariness that is inspirational. That the heart of the home – the kitchen – is the place where so many women's stories are told, happen, and borne witness to. To share ordinary women's voices, to empower and inspire other women, to tell their stories, and use their voice. Just as we season our food for our bodies, we season our love and self for the soul – Storytelling From The Kitchen!

For centuries we as women were the storytellers. The ones who held the heartbeat of humanity in their souls. Storytelling is the heartbeat of humanity, through it, we pass down knowledge, build up, support, and share traditions, and create vibrant narratives and communication. Women were respected, worshiped, honored, and listened to. They held the knowledge to pass on to future generations, they built trust and communities, and they shared wisdom and heritage. Then came a corruption in the masculine energy, then came the witch trials, then came the silence of women. Our tongues were cut from our mouths, and we were turned against each other. Women were no longer equal in any way to men.

Bringing women together to create a book of empowerment and inspiration aims to be an inspiration for other women to begin to use their voice. It all starts with one word, one sentence and then we will be SHE ALOUD – just hear our roar!

So welcome to Seasoned With Empowerment, buckle up and enjoy the ride as you experience a rollercoaster of emotions, experiences, and triumphs.

SEASONED WITH EMPOWERMENT

Introduction

Let there be no mistake that women are silenced every day. Within these pages, eleven women have come together to take you on a journey from silence and fear to telling their story and empowerment. Please take the time before reading each women's story to absorb the quotes, words, and phrases of silenced voices. These are real women's experiences and feelings. Only then move on to the stories of everyday women leading everyday lives. At the end read the quotes, words, and phrases of empowered voices, this is the result of unlocking your voice.

You will find eleven different voices, from a variety of cultures and backgrounds. Each chapter has been left in the voice of the woman. You may find different spellings as we have both UK, US, and international English. What you will find is story after story of extraordinary women finding ways to overcome adversity, trauma, pain, and misogyny. Each voice has linked the heart of the home, the kitchen, to the heart of humanity, storytelling. The result is empowering and insightful - Storytelling From The Kitchen.

Some voices' stories are intricately intertwined with the kitchen, others share a memory of food and the connection to their story, all share a recipe, tradition, or ritual around food and the kitchen.

Trigger Warning

Before you begin, please be aware that within these pages the authors' voices can be heard in their raw truth. This truth is their story, their experience, their feelings. You will find stories of loss, domestic violence, sexual assault, and other topics that can be triggering or uncomfortable to read. You will not find sensualisation or shock tactics, just women's voices telling their stories. Not all voices were silenced by big traumas, but their silence and journey are as valid as those who were. Some voices were always loud but evolved to share new truths and reinvent themselves to follow the path of their dreams. Each voice is empowered.

Our hope for you, the reader, is that you too can begin to tell your story.

WALL OF SILENCE

SHE WAS ASKING FOR IT

YOU'RE NOT GOING OUT DRESSED LIKE THAT!

Rape

Be quiet

You're a tease

FRIDGID

BE A GOOD LITTLE GIRL

Girls don't... Go to university, be engineers, do science, work on building sites...

SHE'S A BIT OF ALRIGHT

Nobody likes you.

Don't embarrass me!

Fatty...skinny...ugly... too much make up...

DOMESTIC VIOLENCE

Don't be so emotional

You're mine. I can do what I like.

Child abuse

You are just a woman, don't get above your station.

WELL WHAT DID YOU EXPECT DRESSED LIKE THAT.

SHE SLEPT HER WAY TO THE TOP

You are too much!

DON'T EXAGGERATE, IT'S NOT THAT BAD

THE AUTHORS

NIXIE FOSTER

JAN OCKENDON

CLAIRE WALSH

LEAH PALMER

JACKIE HALL

LISA WILLIAMS

KALLIA PAPADOPOULOS

MANDY NICHOLSON

DANI SMITH

EL JEDRAS

GRACE FULLER

CHAPTER TITLES

NIXIE FOSTER

Nixie is a Storyteller, Illustrator, Author, and Founder of Holistic Storytelling Publishing House and the movement S.H.E. Aloud. She heals the whole and empowers women by unlocking their voices through books, writing, workshops, journalling, podcasts, talks, and more.

Her mission is to create inclusive communities bringing women and feminine beings together and reignite the power of storytelling. Her vision is to help women unlock their voices to create empowerment, archives, and immersive experiences accessible to all, creating a world that is better and does better for women.

DO YOU REMEMBER THE GIRL WITH THE WIND IN HER HAIR?

I was once a girl who knew the power of the wind in her hair and the warmth of the sun upon her skin. I was once a girl who knew how to be. Not what she should be. Not how she should be. Not what she was expected to be. A girl who knew just how to be. This girl was alive. This girl was authentic. This girl shone from the light in her eyes to the magical sparks that left a trail as she walked. This girl was me. This girl could have been you or a hundred other girls.

Do you remember her?

I do!

I remember letting the wind blow me across the playground. I remember how it filled me with joy and the sound of the laughter all around as child after child gleefully connected with Mother Nature at that moment. From the exceedingly small to the almost tall, boy and girl, we embraced the excitement the wind brought. We flung our arms wide and faced the wind as the first nip of winter bit the air. Being blown across that playground was just the best feeling. Some of us wore our coats like capes, and others untied their hair to whip against their faces, and others who normally stood and stared joined in. The differences between us all forgot in the sheer joy that Gaia, Mother Earth, brought with the strong October winds. Until the big people came, the teachers running and shouting, 'Stop that', 'Girls get inside before your skirts blow up', 'Boys don't rip your coats'.

I remember warm summer nights when nothing mattered but being together as a family. The gentle breeze from the beach, sandcastles built like cars, holes dug to fill with water, and shells collected. A carefree time when nothing but the moment existed. Walking home from the holiday clubhouse with my dad and a bag of chips looking at the stars. How he showed me the bright light of the north star and the big dipper. My excitement as for two weeks we watched the moon wax or wane. A time when I was just me and nothing else. The warm smell of sea and sand, and the quiet night sounds will always be anchors of happiness for me.

I remember back further sitting at the kitchen table with paint and water making butterfly after butterfly. I folded the paper just the way my mum had shown me. My small hands getting covered in paint, the water spilling, and the big smile and praise for work well done. It didn't matter that I had made a mess, it didn't matter that some just weren't quite right, it didn't matter, I was creating and having fun. The smell of cabbage cooking and the flowery apron my mum had tied around her waist. Always a memory to bring a smile to my face.

All of these were moments before I had become small. All moments before I understood that to shine my light wasn't really what I should do. It wasn't really what good little girls did. These were moments before I began to untrust myself. Before I questioned if I was right. Before the answers had to come from outside of me.

What memories are yours before that time when you no longer could just be?

Can you remember them still?

I don't know exactly when my voice fell silent because for all to see I was loud and confident, but I was good at putting on the masks society handed out to all the girls. Inside I was crying, screaming, withering, becoming so much less than me. The mask I took was not the good little girl who sat in the corner looking pretty, nor was it the studious one who used her brains to become a doctor, lawyer, teacher, nurse, or any other way the good girl could change the world. The mask I took was the one held up to us to show how not to be, the one that was portrayed as wrong, and most definitely not the one that a good little girl chose.

For me, the silencing of my voice began when the inside was big and the outside was small. When all my dreams had no doubts attached to them. It was at first in the whispers from teachers, family, and friends who smiled at my dreams at my fierceness. The ones who labelled me shy when really, I just didn't have anything to say. I was a watcher, a former of ideas that they wouldn't have wanted to hear. Then came the time to choose a future that followed the expectations of society and a personal life that was meant to be a dream. Only mine didn't; I wanted to draw, write, talk, and create to change the world, to make it a better place. And then to top it all one of the clever girls from a good family got pregnant and she hadn't finished school; that was me. I had ruined my life, embarrassed my mum, it was time to stop messing around with all the silliness that had supposedly destroyed me and knuckle down.

The fierce lioness that took no shit, who followed her dreams and was going to change the world withered and died. The cage was complete around my soul and heart, the key turned and the door slammed shut. The voices inside no longer shouted with pride but in despair they cried. The echoes of useless, undeserving, disgusting, ruined, jinxed, and unworthy rung inside my head. Then came the time when these echoes became cemented in stone. I found a man who loved me, who wanted to possess and own me. I ran to his open arms and gratefully took refuge there. These arms were deceptive though; they were not open to hug and hold and heal the broken parts of me. Oh no! They were there to crush those last remaining parts of me and to turn even the echoes into dust. What followed was over a decade of domestic violence. I was left questioning if I even truly existed. There were times it felt like I was a shadow or a ghost who was fleetingly seen but didn't actually exist.

The day I broke and howled in pain was the night of a full moon. Under her light and with a rose quartz clasped in my hand I found the strength to say no, no more. I know if I had stayed, I would not be here today and I am grateful for the strength that I had anchored in the moon long ago as a small child. The key turned in the lock that day to free my soul but more was to come before I healed back to me. It would be years later when I became a mum for the second time to my long-wished-for son.

I birthed my son and entered a new period of my life, my true motherhood, my new rite of passage. My journey of matrescence began. How unaware, how unprepared, how unsure I was! Now I needed answers: where would I look? I didn't look to the place inside of me, I still didn't trust my intuition, instead, I looked for the answers outside of me. You would have thought I had learned by now, but still, my voice was just a whisper.

What gadgets do I need?
What brand should I use?
How should I do things?
When should things be done?
What am I aiming for and when?

So many questions and doubts flew around inside my head instead of listening to the knowledge that dwelled deep inside. A feeling of judgment, a hidden shame, and these seeds of doubt were sown; the seed of not being a good enough mum. Then came a revolution, I called bullshit, bollocks, and what a load of fuckery. The answer I discovered is inside of me! In the depths where the untrusted knowing began calling to be heard, shouting at me - I can trust me - I can learn to be. It was time to unlearn - relearn - reconnect to that girl of memories in a time when it was ok to just be. The feminine intuition and the maternal instincts; these are to be trusted, they are the switch that lights the beacon. Then I began my journey to be the mother I thought and dreamt of, the mother I truly wanted to be.

It was not a short journey and I had much healing, and still do, to do. There are moments when I let the fear and past traumas take over. But each time my voice becomes stronger as I heal and unlock another cage, release another part of the musical score that is my voice. Reconnecting to my dreams of changing the world through art, writing, and voices has been a big part of this. Reigniting the fire to give women voices through Stories, Heard, Empower has been the biggest key to unlocking those final doors. Women are the keepers of knowledge and we will be the teller of stories once again as our voices become heard.

It is time to heal yourself and fill your vessel - then it is time to shine in true goddess fashion and be who you were born to be.

Food Memory

It was along my journey that I realised how much of my story's backdrop was the kitchen. It was a safe place and a place that fed my heart, soul, and body. I have many stories that I could tell but one encompasses the whole. A family tradition for our birthdays was to choose the takeaway we wanted to order, or the restaurant that we wanted to eat at. I would swing from going out to an Italian or having a Chinese takeaway at home. One year I just didn't want to. I can't remember why, I know I didn't want to have to sit and talk to my family and didn't feel like I deserved to celebrate. But my wonderful dad had other ideas. He was a chef in a former career and I remember the wonderful meals he created but this one will always stand out, Nikki's Spareribs. Spareribs were my favourite part of a Chinese takeaway and he knew there was something wrong. He wanted to show me I mattered in the only way he knew how through the magic of the kitchen. He created a dish just for me. This then became the dish that I wanted and he cooked for my birthday every year. When I became estranged from my parents during the decade of domestic violence, I thought I would never taste that dish again.

We lost my parents within a year of each other during the time of the pandemic, not to covid. Clearing out their home I kept some of the recipe books of both my mum's and dad's. I began to go through things to pack for my house move to a place where I would be beginning again and building the life I truly wanted. I was excited but also nervous too. I had already begun working on the project to bring women's voices together and show the link between the heart of the home and the heart of humanity – the kitchen and storytelling. All of this combined kept me swinging between knowing for certain and letting all the old trauma and doubts creep in about myself. When what fell out from between the pages of one of the books but the recipe for Nikki Style Spareribs. I took this as a sign of being loved, an affirmation to trust myself, and comfort. This is the recipe I want to share with you. I will be making these every year on my birthday.

Nikki Style Spareribs

Ingredients

3lb Spareribs

2oz crystallised ginger

1 large onion

3 cloves of garlic

A generous sprig of each – mint, oregano, rosemary, and parsley

½ teaspoon paprika

Pinch of cajon pepper (hot)

4 tablespoons white wine vinegar

6 tablespoons olive oil

6 tablespoons sunflower or vegetable oil

Salt and pepper to taste

Method

Blend onion, garlic, and fresh herbs (in blender).

Add salt and pepper.

Leave blender running and slowly add white wine vinegar and oils.

Put ribs in a glass bowl and pour marinade over.

Leave for 24 hours in a fridge stirring occasionally.

Cooking

Preheat oven to gas mark 3.

Put in a large baking dish and cover with foil.

Cook for 1 ½ hours stirring occasionally.

Remove from oven.

Finely chop crystalised ginger and add.

Adjust seasoning if necessary.

Return to the oven without foil increasing oven to gas mark 4.

Cook for a further 45 mins or until golden brown.

Serve with rice it is delicious!

I have copied exactly what was written down by my Mum for Dad's recipe. A little bit of both of them preserved and to keep as a part of our family heritage.

Join me on a journey of empowerment by connecting with me here:

SHE Aloud Podcast

Apple Podcasts
Spotify
Amazon Music

The Holistic Storytelling Community
https://www.facebook.com/groups/holisticstorytellingcommunity

Website
https://www.nixiefoster.com

Books On Amazon
The Story of the Gonks

Little Moon's Samhain Adventure

Moon Gazing Empowerment Journal

Love & light
Nixie

JAN OCKENDON

Jan is a Psychotherapist and coach working with women to rediscover and embrace their inner feminine power. Using the female cycles, the menstrual cycle through to menopause. Jan has a special interest in perimenopause, seeing this as an opportunity for women to blossom into the wild woman they were always meant to be.

She has over 30 years of experience as a mental health nurse, psychotherapist, and now spiritual life coach. With all the knowledge and skills that brings along with her own life experiences, Jan can create what is needed to help the woman sat in front of her at any time.

Covid Was Just What I Needed

I had Covid just as we were put into lockdown for the first time, it was horrible. I am very rarely ill, so it was a complete shock to be knocked off my feet like that. I couldn't even remember the last time I had flu it was so long ago. I've had it again since, but it wasn't so bad, both times for my birthday though. Whose idea of a gift was that then?

Turns out it was a gift even if I didn't recognise it at the time. The world standing still and then moving online has opened more doors for me than being in a "normal" world for years ever did. Come with me and I'll explain.

I always felt a bit alone. Not that I didn't have friends, but I also always felt like it wasn't quite right. Sitting in my bedroom playing and wondering what was coming next. Imagine the girl sat staring into space, what's in her head and where is she in her imagination right now. I actually can't tell you because I can't remember. Oh, but the boys whispering, "inflatable tits" and the old women in the shops telling my mum I looked "just like Shirley Temple". From the bullying that gets passed off as "banter" to full-on sexual harassment/abuse, how would I keep his hands off me in science class this week? I often sat in my teens dreaming of leaving home and going off to a showjumping or eventing yard to work with the horses there. I loved horses, their soft, warm muzzles that smelled so good and always made me feel better when they tickled my hand with their whiskers. So, I lost confidence, not just in having dreams but in who I was. I was told often, "You never keep going at anything", and "you never finish what you start". One of the things I was told was that I never kept trying at things and I gave up if I wasn't good at it straight away or that I was a disruptive influence. Did anyone ever wonder why I got bored quick or tried to amuse myself in class? I've believed my whole life that I was just crap, but now I know that's not true. I hadn't found what I was looking for yet.

What do you do when you leave school believing you'll never be able to have what you really want? Never get to reach your dreams. That girl sat on the horse in the indoor school, with a fabulous seat but no confidence in her own ability. Telling everyone she prefers to do all the stable work and not the riding when the riding was what she lived for. That feeling of power from the horse and the energy but wait, she wasn't ever going to make it though, right? I was so anxious about it that I did give up in the end.

Next thing to try then? Mental health nursing, I couldn't go too far wrong with that, could I? My mum told me one of the things she'd always liked about me was I always wanted to stand up for the underdog. I started training in the 1980s and the stigma about having a mental health problem was huge then. Is it possible to care too much? I'm not sure anymore at this point in my life, I did think if it was then I did! For a while anyway, then who knew it was so easy to switch off the caring to protect yourself? I found out quite quickly I couldn't work like that, especially in nursing homes. All those residents were someone's mum, dad, or grandparent. How could you not feel something for them? Things got tougher and I had to get out, we all think we can change things from the inside don't we but sometimes the little fish just gets pulled along in the wake of the bigger fish, and their voice gets drowned out.

Then along came children, mine, and other peoples who I looked after as a childminder. Children are amazing, watching them play together or play alongside each other is fabulous. I didn't know what was wrong with me though because here I was doing what I wanted to do, I had even sent my husband a letter years before saying that's what I was going to do when we had kids, but I was feeling crap. I still couldn't speak up and felt really fed up. I still didn't feel like I could speak up enough which when you're working with parents as well as the kids is not ideal.

Shall I go back to nursing? It's what I knew, right? It's actually what I was good at, wasn't it? Thing is I wasn't sure anymore, but something had to change. Everything changed when I qualified, did my nurse training, and went to university. Ooh, university, me. That girl the head of sixth form said couldn't stay on to A levels because she was disruptive and now, she's here at The University of Leeds. So much learning to come, over the next few years in hospitals which has shaped who I am now. Cradle to Grave was the original strap line of the NHS and I did that. Oh, and the university thing. Well, let's just say I loved it. Who knew studying could become a bit addictive? Especially after being told, it wasn't my thing for so long. If you read some of my assignments you might agree, but I came out with a good enough degree to also get on a masters level psychotherapy course. That fear again though, stopped me at post-grad diploma after a disappointment with one piece of work.

As I write this now, looking back at the journey I've been on I can feel the tears always close. It's been easy to feel like a solo traveller which has been hard over the years. You know what though? A big discovery, I am pretty good at cooking and baking. Oh, my goddess, the fun in the kitchen over the years. Brought people to our house often too, the alchemy of mixing together a few ingredients with a whole heap of love and baking them to bring people together. Who doesn't love cake as well? The smell of baking in our house was always commented on by neighbours who often said they wanted to make up a reason to come around. Ooh, the feel of kneading bread too. Adult playdough anyone? That feel of the dough squidging between my fingers, I love it. The best bit though is how it brings people together and because everyone wants something different, I get to bake more. Hoorah! When I bake I get lost in the smells, texture, and feel of what's in front of me and forget about everything else. It can be a real mindful moment or quite a few moments really and its effect doesn't just make me feel good it helps give others a sweet treat too.

Back to Covid and how it helped me to get to where I am now. Remember what I do? I used to love going to the gym, walking, or running on the treadmill. BUT here I was reaching the point of burn out, running like a hamster in a wheel just to keep my head above water. Covid got me just before the first lockdown and I was quite ill, so it forced me to stop and be still for a while. I think the whole world had that opportunity to just stop the busyness and running round that we were all doing. I held my breath a bit when it came to going back to work. Not because I don't like the work I do; it was the thought of the commuting again. It's not the getting up early, anyone who knows me will tell you I'm up at 5.30 most days. It was leaving the house early, having to be "professional" whatever the fluff that is and fit into dress codes that someone else thinks are right.

Stopping the treadmill meant I was also able to find a tribe of women who have become friends and remind me who I am regularly. Women who support each other and don't pull each other down to feel better about themselves. Finding Mums in Business International during the first lockdown in the UK brought some of those amazing women into my life. All this helped me to find my own voice again and remember my spirituality. I know "finding your voice" means different things to different people. To me it means being able to feel into the deep inner knowing of who I am, not who I have been told I "Should" be. The intuitive knowing when something feels right or wrong. That's difficult to hear when you're running around chasing a dream that isn't your own. I know I always felt a niggle that something wasn't quite right, and it was easy to blame that on not having enough money, not having the right car/job/things/home. All the things we're led to believe are the most important things in life but they're really not. The most important things in life come from within and I think that starts with your own voice.

The thing with finding your voice and being able to tell your own truth also means you get to create your reality. Ever heard of a recipe book therapist/coach? Let me ask you this then. Are you exactly the same as your siblings or friends? Do you like the same things, do the same things, or even smell the same. Probably not, right? When I say I am a bit of a recipe book therapist and coach I mean I work with the person sat in front of me on that particular day. Which might mean bringing a different flavour to my therapy or coaching each session. Like I wouldn't bake one cake and expect everyone to love it, I also know that when I cook something I've cooked a thousand times it tastes different each time. That's because when I cook anything I adapt it to suit the people eating it or the ingredients I've got in the fridge and cupboard. I know it will be exactly as it's supposed to be that day though. I rarely use a cookie cutter to cut my cookies so why would I want all my clients to want the same shape therapy? Just like my brownies need really dark chocolate and lots of butter – well it would be an alternative from me as I'm vegan, and not need a lot of beating. One client might need me to be a bit more gentle and encouraging but the next one might need me to be a bit more direct or straightforward in my approach. I wonder if anyone follows a recipe to the exact letter of what's written down. I might follow a formula with baking, you need certain ingredients to make a cake or bread rise and be light, but you can alter the flavouring without it harming the end result. I think the way I work is a bit like that, I know that there are certain things we all need but don't want to admit. I believe the art or alchemy of working with people is knowing when to add a bit of spice for warmth or a bit of sugar to sweeten the work. Or when to be a bit more vanilla, subtle, and warm but enhancing the flavour of everything else. Who knew you could compare therapy and coaching to baking a cake?

I needed a bit of breathing space and was struggling to see where it would come from. So, thank you Covid for bringing what was really needed and helping me find what I needed to unlock my voice.

Footnote:

Although it was lockdown that set the wheels in motion for finding a business that lights up my life it was embracing my spirituality that set me free. Learning to listen to and use my inner voice as well as the signs I'd been seeing and hearing all my life. It was being able to do that which helped me to find a tribe of amazing women who accept me and celebrate me for what I am. All of which has allowed me to be the person I am now and to let go of past energies that were keeping me stuck.

Food Memory

I spent quite a lot of time with my nana when I was young. Nana baked; her pastry was so short it just melted in your mouth. She used to make her version of corned beef hash pie; her corned beef hash was corned beef mashed with potatoes. Anything with mashed potatoes works for me, in fact, I'm sure she made a cheese pie with mashed potato too. The other thing I remember her for was Christmas cake but I'm sure she baked other things as well. I remember she had quite cold hands a lot of the time because people used to say the rhyme "cold hands, warm heart" and she definitely did for me. I was always told cold hands were a must for pastry so I didn't think I'd be any good at it but whatever my nana's actual skill was I seem to have got it and I love making pastry.

One of my best memories was not about home baking at all. My nana lived around the corner from a fabulous shop that had cream cakes and flowers. The ladies in there always spoilt me and cooed over me, I remember often being given one of those round "truffle" cakes that are covered in sprinkles which is probably where I first started to love cake.

My mother-in-law was also a baker, she always had cake in the house. When you went round for tea the table was always heaving under the weight of food piled on it. A lot of which was cake, so it was no surprise our house was rarely without cake for a long time too. I once beat her in a Swiss roll baking class at a local craft show which was possibly not the best move but baking is my happy place and I wanted to share it.

Chocolate Orange Cake

One of the cakes I bake the most is a chocolate orange cake. I'm vegan and allergic to egg as well so everything I bake is vegan even if I know I'll not have much of it. I've tried to perfect vegan brownies and one day I'll do it because all of our family love a brownie but before that, it will always be chocolate orange cake. My favourite cake recipe book is by Ms Cupcake, and I've adapted her recipe to suit my family so here it is: -

Preheat your oven to 180C/350F/gas mark 4 and grease your tins. I never bake cake in a fan oven, I think it dries them out so if you've got a conventional oven go for that.

Greased tins – I use two 8" because I love a deep cake, but you could use two 9". I also use a cake release spray for greasing because it's easier and I line the tin with baking parchment.

340g self-raising flour
60g cocoa powder
240g caster sugar
2tsp baking powder
400ml "milk" I use soya or oat because that's what we have in
160 ml of some sort of flavourless oil – we usually have one that's marked vegetable oil (they're often actually rapeseed oil)
1 tablespoon of orange extract (please don't use essence, it's icky and won't give you the same flavour)
The zest of one orange

You will also need a portion of buttercream (vegan obvs!), chocolate orange version of your favourite recipe.

Method

Take a big bowl and mix up the dry ingredients and the orange zest until they're well combined.

Then add all the wet ingredients – milk, oil, and extract.

Mix carefully until it's all mostly combined but don't over-mix.

Give the bowl a gentle bang on the worktop so the raising agent doesn't work too quickly and divide the mixture between the two tins and bake for about 18-20 minutes depending on your oven.

If it's a bit too squishy still leave it for another 5 mins.

Cool in the tins for as long as you like – the book says 10-15 minutes, but I do sometimes leave them a bit longer because I very rarely do as I'm told.

Cover one cake in buttercream and add the other on the top then cut a big slice and fill yer boots, enjoy with a mug of steaming tea.

Source:

Ms Cupcake, "Turkish Delight Cake." Recipe. *The Naughtiest Vegan Cakes In Town.* London, Square Peg

Please do connect with Jan Ockendon here:
https://www.facebook.com/janockendon

https://www.instagram.com/janockendon

https://www.facebook.com/groups/thewayofthewildwoman

With lots of love

Jan

CLAIRE WALSH

Claire is a stereotype smashing author, writing coach, reader, writer, and proud word-nerd. She is living her lifetime dream of being a writer. The opening paragraph to the story of her life would go something like this…

"Once upon a time there was a little girl who loved to read. She had a tricky time growing up but eventually became a teacher. Over 20 years she read many, many books to many, many children. With each book she read she dreamed of writing her own stories, stories to help little people believe that they can be who they want to be."

Claire made this dream come true and now writes books for children and adults.

As an author, and a writing coach, Claire spends her time writing and encouraging others to write and fulfil their writing dreams.

Wise and Wonderful Women

We are blessed to have five generations of wonderful women in my family.

My grandmother, Nanny Vi, celebrates her 100th birthday in October 2023. She still lives alone in her home and is the most independent person I know.

My mum, in her 70s, wonderful, strong, solo-parent for most of my life, an inspiration for how to live your life your way and not let society tell you that you need a man to validate your existence.

Me, living life to the full, in my 50s, widowed in my 40s with a strong belief that I am still here for a reason and the best tribute I can pay to him is to live my best life.

My daughters, two of them, in their 20s and 30s, strong, smart, beautiful, and brave, they have thrived despite the enormous challenges they have both faced.

My granddaughter, about to hit her teens, sassy and smart, talented, and tenacious. They say it takes a village to raise a child and she is a credit to the village who raised her, and of course, a credit to herself, who she is, and the choices she makes.

Five generations of women, the oldest born in 1923, and the youngest born in 2010, all have faced adversity, yet all are resilient and have thrived and they are not alone.

When I decided to get involved in this project, I knew that it was going to be about women and the experiences that we have shared, in the kitchen and beyond. I love the title of the book, Seasoned with Empowerment, as that's what each of those generations has done for each other, through cooking and chatting, through sharing old traditions, whilst embracing new ideas, through raising each other up, even when we might not always agree.

This is my story. It's a story of intergenerational, unconditional love and support, across the generations. It's a story of resilience when faced with adversity.

So, who am I? Well, I'll start by telling you who I am now, I'm Claire, stereotype-smashing author, reader, writer, and proud word-nerd. I'm a writing coach who empowers other women to embrace their creativity and believe in themselves as writers. I'm a mother, grandmother, widow, and wife.

But that's not who I have always been. My childhood was a tricky time, I didn't have the easiest of childhoods, that's for sure. Growing up in the 1970s wasn't all just choppers, flares, and The Bay City Rollers! We were an ordinary working-class family, living on a council estate in South-East London.

Well, I thought we were ordinary and normal. It wasn't until much later, as a teenager, that I realised not everyone's dad drank so much and went missing for days, even weeks on end, and not everyone's mum cried so much.

Now I want to say at this stage that I love both my dad and my mum very much. But writing is my truth and for me, that means warts and all, without the need to rewrite history. Both my mum and my dad have their flaws, don't we all, but they also have both supported me and loved me. I love them very much, especially now that I'm older and wiser, and reflect on my life.

We weren't rich, in fact, we were poor; even poorer because of my dad's addiction. Financially that is. But gosh we were rich in love. I never had any doubt that my mum and my dad loved me. Grandparents – Theresa and Ted, on my dad's side, Vi and Eric, my mum's parents. Whatever chaos might be happening at home, safety could always be found at my grandparents' houses. A calmness existed there that stopped any feelings of panic. I felt safe, cared for, and cherished.

I remember so much love and adoration. I felt so much love, even amongst the times of chaos. My grandparents were always there. Steadfast and strong, showing me that love was guaranteed and I could feel safe and protected when I was with them. Fear was banished, and of course, there was always something delicious and nutritious to eat. I remember vividly my grandad Ted's speciality. Yellowy, browny in colour, spongy, cake-like, and pointed, almost triangular! We called them Mexican hats. Grandad Ted's Yorkshire puddings. Unlike any other Yorkshire pudding you will have ever tasted or seen. Was it that he made them with powdered egg, a throwback from rationing during the war? Was it that he made them with love? I don't know, but I do know they made my taste buds tingle, especially after that Sunday roast, because he always made twice as much as we needed. Why? you might ask. For pudding of course! Cut open and spread with butter and sprinkled with sugar! A poor person's dessert, they were the best.

Anyway, I digress! That often happens when I think of food! So, what of those wonderful women in my family? Let me introduce you to the women who made me the woman I am today.

Nanny Theresa, the foulest mouth you would ever hear. She swore like a docker, Grandad Ted was a docker, yet I don't remember him swearing! She had a foul mouth, smoked roll-ups, and had a dirty, infectious laugh. I grew up thinking 'fucking' was an adjective because she used it so much! Her voice wasn't silenced it was loud, lairy, and very fucking sweary! She had survived a war and was scared of nothing. Fiercely protective of her family, she was one of my biggest champions when I became the first person in our family to go to university. "Go get an ology" she said, like in the adverts (if you are old enough to remember). Only I didn't get an ology the first time around. I got pregnant. OOooppps! Again, she remained on my side, proud as punch, when I gave birth to my eldest daughter. A solo-parent before my daughter was two, she and Grandad Ted supported me, including when I returned to university with a two-year-old in tow. She supported me emotionally, physically, and financially when times were tough. We shared a love of books and right from being a teenager, she would let me read her vast collection of novels. Although sometimes she would say, not that one yet, you're too young. Usually, if they were steamy and spicy! After I had read a book, we would discuss it and have our own little book club before I even knew book clubs were a thing. The night before she died I sat by her bed and she tried to give me her sapphire ring. We knew she was dying, but I wasn't as comfortable with death as I am now and I couldn't bear the thought of losing her. I refused to take the ring. To take it would have meant accepting the inevitable. I wasn't ready to accept that. The next morning was my 24th birthday. I awoke to the news she had died and I regretted not taking the ring and saying thank you. I regretted not accepting she was going to die and telling her it was okay, I loved her very much. To this day I still sometimes finish a book and want to talk to her about it.

Nanny Vi, our queen, our matriarch, 99 years old, and quite simply the most amazing woman you would want to meet. Like me she was widowed early in life, my Grandad Eric dying while I was still at primary school. He was a legendary fancy dress costume maker, and we were always winning fancy dress competitions thanks to his designs! Nanny Vi worked in the print industry and had fought hard for her right to work as a mother in a generation when women were expected to stay at home and be 'just' housewives. My mum recalls my Grandad Eric saying 'You'll last 6 weeks' when she got her first job. She worked until well into her 70s and showed us not only that as women we could be mothers and work, but also gave us a great work ethic.

My Mum, what a woman! She tried as hard as she could to protect us kids from the addiction and the horrors that went with it, whilst being as loving and supportive as she could to my dad, understanding that his addiction was an illness. Her and my dad got back together after divorcing as my dad had had a sustained dry period and really seemed to get his drinking under control. This resulted in a surprise, beautiful, baby sister when I was 15. The sober period didn't last though and so she was a solo parent to 3 children and working full-time. A hero!

My mum was brave and left my dad several times, and during these periods we would often move into Nanny Vi's house, my mum's childhood home. I remember these times so fondly; it was such a time of calmness and contentment. Nanny Vi would throw a sheet over her dining room table and my brother and I would play dens. I would of course usually snuggle with a book whenever I could.

I remember we ate a lot of turkey and chicken! My mum and nan were frequently watching their weight so would buy a bird and make it last all week. Roast on Sunday, delicious, moist, and tasty, with salad throughout the week, and even soup made from the carcass.

Sometimes we had money, sometimes we didn't, but as with many working-class families, there were plenty of ideas for making money go further. Bread pudding for example. Not that milky pasty mess, but proper South London bread pudding. A deep brown, fruit-filled, moist, and crunchy sweet sensation. No measuring, no weighing, just a great way to use up leftover bread and fill rumbling tummies with a tasty treat.

Mince and mash. Not quite as delicious as bread pudding, especially when the cheapest of meat was all we could afford. Grey and grisly! Yuk. But herbs and veg and a pinch of that special ingredient, love, and suddenly it was delicious. Everything tastes better with love – even caviar. I remember once at primary school, in maths, doing bar charts on what we had for breakfast that day. The look on the teacher's face when I replied "caviar on toast!" Not your usual working-class family breakfast. But we had a mountain of the stuff – I found out as an adult it was some sort of dodgy deal as it had fallen off the back of a lorry. I can't stand the stuff now!

But whatever was on the menu, I remember lots of love and lots of encouragement. I was brought up to believe that I could be anything. I could be whoever I want. I was raised to have an opinion and to speak that opinion loud and clear. I was born to have a voice and I was entitled to be heard. I will never be able to thank my mum and the women in my life enough but I have gone on to make sure my daughters and granddaughter know just the same.

So, five generations of wonderful women with voices that are there to be heard. It's not always easy, it is usually very loud, but it is seasoned with empowerment and love!

Food Memory

As mentioned in my chapter, food played a big part in my life and still does. I have such fond memories about the feast that was Christmas dinner.

We would always have big family Christmases, taking it in turns to host, with temporary tables set up to accommodate the different generations and different households around the table. That table would be laden with food, everyone would chip in bringing what they could. Saving stamps we collected throughout the year were cashed in to make sure that it was a meal to remember.

There was always a turkey of course and it was usually joined by some other meat, sometimes a gammon, sometimes beef. Plenty of potatoes, usually cooked in a couple of different ways, mashed roast, or even dauphinoise. More vegetables in one meal than we would usually have in a week, carrots, brussels, cauliflower, parsnips, red cabbage, the choice was immense. And of course, the sauces, gravy, bread sauce, cranberry sauce, mint sauce even if there wasn't lamb.

And that's just the main course, the starter was usually a prawn cocktail or soup. Christmas pudding, of course, mince pies, and a wonderful trifle. Christmas was a special time, and we sure knew how to celebrate; and still do!

Family Tradition

You won't be surprised to know that this tradition involves food and books. Christmas Day in my household starts with Green Eggs and Ham. No, not the book by Dr Seuss, but my top-secret recipe for gammon, which I cook on Christmas Eve. On Christmas morning, after presents have been opened, it is sliced, fried, and served with eggs. I don't know when it began to be called green eggs and ham, and my children are convinced that it really used to be green, but no, just delicious gammon and eggs, although I once found green ketchup to serve with it!

Recipe

Bread Pudding

Oh, so many to choose from! I'm going to go with Bread Pudding! No weighing and measuring is needed, just go with whatever you have to hand, and it will be delicious.

You will need:
Some stale bread, a great way to use it up when it's past its best but not yet mouldy! A recipe would probably say around 500g, but I just add in whatever I have. Sometimes I even add in other stale bakery items such as bagels and rolls!

A selection of dried fruit, mixed peel, and some nuts. Again, I just use whatever I have around.

Cinnamon, or mixed spice, or both!
Milk – about half a pint but depends on how much bread you have.
Two or three eggs, beaten.
A knob of butter melted.
A few tablespoons of sugar.

It's so easy you just need to tear the bread into pieces and chuck it in a big bowl. Add all the other ingredients, mix and squish together so the bread becomes moist, and the mixture is like a cake mixture. Add more milk if it's too dry and let it all soak together for about 15 mins.

Heat the oven to about 180c. Put the mixture into a greased tin, I prefer a square one. If you have any brown sugar, you could sprinkle the top of the mixture. Cover with foil and bake for about an hour. Take the foil off and bake for around another half hour until firm and golden.

Mmmmmm delicious, my mouth is watering as I type. Enjoy!

You can order Claire's books here:
The Princess Without a Crown : Walsh, Claire, Farrer, Jayne: Amazon.co.uk: Books

The Pink Widow: Amazon.co.uk: Walsh, Claire: 9781912677917: Books

Please reach out and connect with Claire here:
Facebook:
Claire Walsh Author
https://www.facebook.com/profile.php?id=100030791694987

The Pink Widow
https://www.facebook.com/ThePinkWidow/

The Write Life with Claire
https://www.facebook.com/groups/116400990378874

And check out her website:
Out Of The Box Books
https://ootb-books.co.uk/

Remember, if you want to be a writer, write!
Love Claire

LEAH PALMER

I'm Leah Palmer, a dyslexic writer at the beginning of my journey.

Reading is a huge passion of mine. I always have a book with me ready to disappear into. It's my joy of reading that I wish to pass on to others, especially children. My niece and nephew inspired me to write my first children's book, due to be published end of 2023. I have written a couple of pieces for adults, a short story called From Dating App to Love, for a writing competition and of course have had the complete pleasure of being part of this amazing collaboration book.

Dyslexia Doesn't Stop Me From Reaching My Dreams

They say the school years are the best days of our lives. We make new friendships some that last a lifetime, you learn skills and knowledge that will be used throughout your life. Yet for me, school wasn't always the best place. My enemies weren't so much the other kids in the playground, mine was the English language, and trying to learn the basic skills needed to conquer some of my biggest foes. Spelling, phonics, phonetic reading, and writing. Every day in class I would hope they wouldn't pick me to demonstrate to the class the word of the day or to phonically sound out the letter of the day. As I sat there my heart would be pounding and my hands would start to sweat, my body would go frigged with fear until someone's name was called out. Yet I would be picked at some point, the embarrassment was awful! As comments of "Leah is stupid" rippled through the class. The embarrassment wasn't to stop there. The teachers decided I was falling behind too much, so special classes were required. "Special Classes" means help for those falling behind, or in kids' translation "Thick Class".

Once a week I would be taken from my classroom and placed with others who were also falling behind. For one hour a week, I would be in these additional classes. I would try my hardest to get things right, yet no matter how hard I tried I just couldn't grasp some of the things they were teaching me. They would always send me home with spellings as weekly homework, then test me the following week. I would get praised for the ones I got correct, the ones I got wrong would be added onto a new list for that week's homework. My praise didn't last long as I was then asked to phonetically read them, which is where things would all go wrong again. This then became the norm for me, every week I would go to my additional classes, and the weeks passed quickly turning into months. Others I had gotten to know had disappeared, gone back to their normal classes, now replaced with new additions. The consistency was me! I never left; I was the constant in the group. I was still trying to figure out why I could not grasp what everyone else found so easy to catch up on.

I do have to thank these classes though, as I can read one word phonetically thanks to them, this word is Wed-Nes-Day (Wednesday). It seems repetition worked on me, and as our classes were always on a Wednesday, this word I have been able to phonetically read since those days, it's one of two words I can read this way.

My teachers took a different route with me when they saw nothing was working and encouraged me to read more. This turned out to be the best thing they could ever have done for me; reading was a challenge to start with as I couldn't always read the words in front of me. The teachers soon realised that phonetical reading wasn't going to work for me, so decided instead to read the word as a whole to me and get me to repeat it back twice. This was how I learned to read! It was just small steps to start with and then they would give me reading homework as well as the spelling.

My parents helped me a lot with my homework tasks. As my reading improved, they even got myself and my sister into the local library to encourage more reading. My grandad also helped a great deal, he would get me to sit with him at the dining room table, and he would give me a children's poetry book or children's book and ask me to read to him. If I ever stopped, he would lean over, tell me the word I was stuck on and get me to repeat it twice before carrying on. Once I was able to read the poem or book all the way through without stopping, he would move on to a new one, this time a little bit more difficult. I loved these times I spent with my grandad, not only did it introduce me to some great authors like C.S Lewis and Laurie Lee to name a few, but also to some great poetry. He also helped me to improve my reading immensely. There would be times when I was reading to him that he would ask me to stop, as it was time to take a break. He would make us both a cup of tea and share a scone with me. As we sat there drinking our tea and eating our scones he would often ask if I was enjoying the piece I was reading. Just thinking back on it now as I write this it brings a smile to my face, and a tear to my eyes, as I remember what a great man he was.

By the time I left primary school, I had caught up with everyone else, thanks to the help of my parents, my grandad, and the additional classes. As I headed into secondary school, I went in a happier young girl then I had felt in primary school. I had more confidence and was determined to do my best. What I didn't realise going in was how my classes would be structured and how this was going to be such a challenge for me.

Some classes I was able to pick up very quickly, yet others I found very difficult. I took two different language classes, one was French and the other was Spanish, yet their teaching techniques could not have been more different. In the French class, you were only allowed to speak French, it was surprising to me how quickly I picked this language up. Yet in Spanish class we were taught English to Spanish, here I really struggled and couldn't really grasp the subject at all. Any classes that were hands on like Woodwork, Cookery, or Textiles etc, I managed to pick up quickly. The theory side of all these classes threw me, I would experience similar situations in other classes such as Religious Education, History, and Maths. I enjoyed these classes immensely as they offered such great insight, yet in all three I struggled with worksheets, questionnaires, and workbooks. No matter how much help I got or asked for they were my Kryptonite! Sending me into a tumble of confusion. I would often ask for help with them and get told "You should know this by now" or "Haven't you been paying attention?". Comments I would hear repeatedly though out the rest of my education and into my adult life.

My biggest enemy of course was English, I have to say I hated this class. I had struggled so much in primary school, so to have to study this language even deeper in secondary school; was like walking into a living nightmare for me. Talking about Nouns, Pronouns, Verbs, Adjectives, and Adverbs was like asking me to compose an opera, I didn't have a clue what they were going on about! No matter how many times we revisited the subject, this was something that wasn't going to register with me.

These classes sent me right back to primary school, it was like I was standing in the middle of the classroom at my desk again, everyone judging me. Fear would come over me every time I was walking into class. I would sit myself at the back, my hands sweaty, hoping I wouldn't get asked to answer any of the questions. It was easier to go unnoticed in secondary school, just copy off the board and hope to God you got the homework right.

There was a class I seemed to excel at, and this was English literature. Since taking up reading it had become my new love, so this class became my favourite. Being introduced to authors such as Shakespeare and Steinbeck was another delight for me. The other thing that was also bought out in me during this time was creativity in writing. Despite my problems with spelling and grammar which were always pointed out, my writing skills improved the more essays and stories they got me to do. It was just unfortunate that it was also to be the last time I would do any writing again for many years.

As I left school and entered the world beyond, it became apparent to me that my difficulties with the English Language and my ability to fully understand it went far beyond the classroom. As I started to apply for jobs, I found that I couldn't always understand the structure of the questions on an application form. I started to doubt my own intelligence! I would repeatedly read the questions and still have no better understanding of them. I would start to convince myself I was stupid! How could I not understand a simple question? I was too afraid to ask for help, as I thought this would only prove how stupid I really was, and that people would start to laugh at me. In the end, I had to give in and with the help of family and friends, every time I had any type of form to fill in, I was able to answer the questions fully, as I was able to go to any of them and ask them to explain the question to me. During these times I don't think any of them realised how embarrassed I felt having to ask for help, it still embarrasses me to this day asking for assistants to fill out a form.

I decided that I needed to try and help myself more, so I took up evening classes. I started by redoing my GCSEs in English and Maths. The teachers were helpful and worked with me to help me understand as much as possible, yet I still failed and couldn't get the C grade I so desperately desired. This made me more determined than ever to pass these courses and I retook them three more times, yet it always led to the same outcome. I started to feel like a failure! More stupid than before, who could fail the same two courses four times? It was at this point the teacher advised me to try doing functioning skills instead. Feeling like I had nothing to lose I went and took English and Maths in functioning Skills passing both first time. After this, I threw myself into courses trying to prove to myself that I had the ability to do it. Some I was able to do and pass with ease, yet others were too difficult and I was asked to leave after falling behind too much.

I started to get frustrated with myself, so I took a break from studying and focused on normal life again. I started to concentrate more on my job, social life, and focusing on myself making sure I had downtime and self-care. Yet there was still that nagging pull within me telling me I shouldn't give up! It was like I had something to prove, not just to others but also to myself. So, with the help of a friend, I signed up for a course with the open university, and my studying journey started again. It was while I was studying at the open university that I received a letter to go and have a dyslexia assessment it came out of the blue and I was quite taken aback. At first, I couldn't fathom why I would need a dyslexia assessment, but as requested I turned up to the appointment to find out it was the university themselves that had requested it. I owe a big thank you to the open university, for they finally gave me an answer.

The dyslexia assessment revealed that I have Moderate Dyslexia with a deficit in Phonological and Visual processing. I cried when I read this, not because I had been told I am dyslexic, but because it was a relief! A relief to know I wasn't stupid like I had led myself to believe, A relief to know that it wasn't down to not wanting to learn, more down to that my brain didn't have the ability to learn everything I wanted it to take in. All this pressure I had placed on myself over the years seemed to start dispersing, it was like a huge weight had been taken off me. Now I could be kinder to myself, I didn't need to prove anything, to anyone, especially to me!

As we all went into the lockdowns for Covid, it made me start journalling as it helped to write my thoughts and feelings down during such a difficult time. It was also during the lockdowns that I started to evaluate my life and the direction I wanted it to go in. When talking to a friend I expressed my keenness for writing but didn't know how to begin. She introduced me to a person who has since become a good mentor and friend. She was running a free writing workshop weekend when we met, I got so much insight from this that I joined her group and signed up for her courses. Through her guidance I have entered writing competitions, looking to publish my first book, and am even taking part in this wonderful collaboration. My confidence has been slowly growing along with my writing abilities. Dyslexia hasn't held me back and should never hold you back. This is just the beginning of my journey, where will yours begin?

Scones at my Grandparents

I always remember when I was young, the smell of nan's baking as I walked into her house. Whether this was pastries, her stew, buns, or scones, it was always a lovely smell that greeted you. My grandad and I often shared a cheese scone when reading together, so it is this recipe I would like to share with you all. As well as a classic scone recipe to be accompanied by either your Cream and Jam or Jam and Cream.

Classic Scones with Jam and Clotted Cream

Ingredients for 8 scones
350g Self-raising flour, plus more for dusting
1tsp baking powder.
¼ tsp salt.
85g butter, cut into cubes.
3tbsp caster sugar.
175ml milk.
1tsp vanilla extract
Squeeze lemon juice
Beaton egg, to glaze.
Jam and Clotted Cream to serve.
Added extra: if you like fruit in your scones add 85g plump sultanas the same time as the caster sugar.

Method

Step 1: Heat the oven to 220C/200C fan/ gas 7. Tip the self-raising flour into a large bowl with the salt and the baking powder, then mix.

Step 2: Add the butter, then rub in with your fingers until the mix looks like fine crumbs, stir in the caster sugar.

Step 3: Put the milk into a jug and heat in the microwave for about 30 secs until warm, NOT HOT. Add the vanilla extract and a squeeze of lemon juice, then set aside for a moment.

Step 4: Put a baking tray in the oven. Make a well in the middle of the dry mix, then add the liquid and combine it quickly with a cutlery knife – it

will seem pretty wet at first.
Step 5: Scatter some flour onto the work surface and tip the dough out. Dredge the dough and your hands with a little more flour, then fold the dough over 2-3 times until it's a little smoother, pat into a round about 4cm deep, take a 5cm cutter (smooth–edged cutters cut more cleanly, giving a better rise) and dip it into some flour. Plunge into the dough, then repeat until you have four scones. You may need to press what's left of the dough back into a round to cut out the other four.
Step 6: Brush the tops with a beaten egg, then carefully arrange on the hot baking tray. Bake for 10mins until risen and golden on the top. Eat just warm or cold on the day of baking, Serve with Jam and clotted cream. If freezing, freeze once cool. Defrost, then put in a low oven (about 160C/140C fan/gas 3) for a few minutes to refresh.

Source:
Immediate Media Company Limited ,2023, *BBC GoodFood,* BBC Studios Distribution, 29/06/23, <bbcgoodfood.com>

Classic Cheese Scones

Ingredients
225g Self-raising flour, extra for dusting.
Pinch of salt.
Pinch of Cayenne pepper.
1tsp baking powder.
55g chilled butter, cut into cubes.
120g mature cheddar, grated.
90-100ml milk, plus 1tbsp for glazing.

Method
Step 1: Heat the oven to 200C/180C fan/gas 6, with a large baking tray inside. Sift the flour, salt, cayenne pepper and baking power into a bowl, then sift again to make sure the ingredients are thoroughly combined.
Step 2: Add the butter to the bowl and combine with your fingertips to

make the breadcrumbs. Sprinkle 100g of the cheese into the breadcrumbs and rub together until evenly distributed. Try not to mix too much as the heat from your hands may start to melt the butter.
Step 3: Make a well in the center of the mixture and add the milk in small amounts combining it with a spatula until you have a fairly soft but firm dough. Do not add all the milk at once as you may not need it all to get the right consistency.
Step 4: lightly flour a surface and pat out the dough to approx. 4cm thick, use a medium cutter, dipping into the floor before plunging into the dough. Then put on a sheet of baking parchment, glaze with a little milk and sprinkle with remaining cheese. Slide onto the hot oven tray.
Step 5: Bake in the oven for 15 -20 mins or until golden brown and cooked through.

Source:

Immediate Media Company Limited ,2023, ***BBC GoodFood,*** BBC Studios Distribution, 29/06/23, <bbcgoodfood.com>

Join Leah Palmer on her journey as an author here:
Instagram
https://instagram.com/leahpalmerauthor?igshid=NGExMmI2YTkyZg==

Facebook
https://www.facebook.com/profile.php?id=100093587336929

Best Wishes
Leah

JACKIE HALL

Jackie is an experienced and dedicated complementary therapist and wellbeing mentor with over 10 years of experience in her field.

Jackie was a shy girl, a people pleaser, who got bullied and was too scared of making mistakes. This had stopped her from being true to herself and silenced her voice. Jackie is now ready to share her story of how she hit rock bottom and found light at the end of the tunnel.

As an anxiety warrior herself, Jackie is passionate in helping and empowering women to overcome their own struggles with anxiety, finding balance, and inner peace.

THERE IS LIGHT AT THE END OF THE TUNNEL

Challenge: Fear of failure
Struggle: Anxiety, OCD, and letting go
Resolution: Moving forward, you have to feel the fear and do it anyway

"What if I fall?
Oh, but my darling,
what if you fly?"
(Erin Hanson)

This is a quote that I can really resonate with. I have always been a little anxious throughout my teenage years and into adulthood. My biggest fear has always been fear of failure.

Struggling to fit in, people pleaser, does that all sound familiar? Coming from a childhood where I switched schools a few times due to my dad being in the army, it has been hard to make friends. I went from a German school to an English school with no communication skills in the English language. Making friends should be easy for children, well for me it wasn't. I was the shy eight-year-old in the background trying to fit in with everyone. Once my language improved, I was able to get noticed more. Unfortunately for the wrong reason.

I was doing silly things, often getting into trouble with my parents, as well as with my teachers. One time that I remember was I got dared to break a pencil in our classroom. You guessed it, I took on the dare and did just that. The teacher noticed it and I got called up in class and told off in front of everyone. I felt humiliated and sad at the same time.

That's when my fear of failure started. I did not want to be told off anymore or get into trouble in any way. Looking back, I know as a child, I should have just taken it with a pinch of salt, but no not Jackie. I continued to shy away from others and just stayed quiet.

During my teens, things were no different. I got bullied at school for being a little different. It was hard and sad when some of your classmates say 'Watch out here comes Jackie, ew Jackie pest, don't touch her' I was so hurt by this comment, but never had the courage to say anything back to them.

Things took their toll, I hid in my room, I self-harmed, and also had an eating disorder. It started with bulimia and soon went into anorexia. This was my way of controlling my emotions.

It was hard as my mum was always at work, I did not have a close relationship with her then, so I felt that I could not speak to her or anyone whom I could trust. Until I met my best friend, Claudia. Luckily, I have managed to overcome my eating disorder and self-harming, quickly.

I was so happy when I got my first job as a trainee practice nurse, which I got at my local GP. I loved my job, I got to meet and communicate with patients, other nurses, and my boss. My shyness had started to ease, and I was more open to communicating with others. My boss was very strict and one thing I remember on my first day that she said to me was 'Don't you know how to greet your boss? You must always shake their hand to leave a good impression and always look into their eyes when you are speaking, or are being spoken to'.

This is something that I will never forget and yes, I do look people in their eyes all the time.

In adulthood I thought that I would be much better, that my communication would improve, wanting to be heard by others, but for the wrong reasons where I was still people-pleasing and trying to fit in, but with the wrong crowd.

Yet again things took a turn for the worse. I lost my job, and my home, and had nowhere to go or turn to. Being homeless was very hard. I did not know where I was going to sleep from one night to the next. I stayed out late drinking, partying, and staying wherever I could. One night, I was supposed to stay at Michelle's house, but she let me down and would not open the door. It was 3 am, so all I could do was stay outside in her doorway. I knew that my grandparents lived close by, so I waited until around 5am and walked to theirs. I knew that they were early birds and should be up very soon. My grandma opened the door and was shocked to see me. I was too afraid to tell her the truth that I had no home. I did however tell her that Michelle had let me down.

I loved my grandparents. The memories that I have of them are precious from when they lived by a farm where we picked sweetcorn, strawberries and had a go at milking cows. My granddad worked on a steam train and sometimes we were allowed to join him on board and pull the train whistle. Grandma played board games with us, although she did not like losing, and I'm sure sometimes she may have even cheated. 'Ha ha,' this has just made me smile. It's good to look back at happy memories, isn't it? Grandma also made the best meals. Oh, just thinking of her dishes makes my mouth water. She was always up early to prepare the meals for the day and stocked up her own homemade jams, pickles, and apple crumbles in their cellar. It was not long after that my grandma became ill and sadly passed away.

As things had still not improved, I called my best friend and she took me in at her parent's house, I was hiding up in their attic until one day her mother found out. She was so helpful and understanding. For the first time, I felt listened to and supported. I was able to stay at their house until I found a place of my own. One thing I loved whilst staying at theirs was her mum's cooking. She was from the Philippines and her dishes were just delicious. To this day I am forever grateful to my best friend and her mum.

Soon after, I started a new job as a pole dancer. Yes, that's right a pole and exotic dancer, you would not have thought that shy Jackie would do a strip dance. Well, I did. I travelled all over Germany and accommodation was provided for me, so I had nothing to lose.

My dream had always been to be a dancer, never did I imagine that I would do this type of dancing. I tell you; this was definitely an eye-opener for me. I saw things that you cannot imagine in this industry. I was asked to do other things, but that certainly was not me, so I decided to leave the industry after just 5 months and travel to the UK to visit my family.

That is when I met my now husband, Darren. It was his humour and charm that got me to fall in love with him. Darren was my auntie's next-door neighbour, he found out that I was a dancer and wanted to meet me. On the day we arranged to meet he brought round a pole and with his humour said 'Come on then, show us your moves'. That just made me laugh, cheeky I thought.

Our relationship started straight away, I also got pregnant quickly, so I decided to stay and live in England and never looked back.

Moving to the UK without any friends, I found very challenging. I was pregnant, my auntie kicked me out of their home (to this day we never understood why), I felt alone, and I was not speaking to my parents who then still lived in Germany. All I had was the support of Darren and his parents. They took me in, and I was able to live with them until we found a place of our own.

As I only just met them, I felt very isolated and stayed hidden away in Darren's bedroom. Not very good for your soul, I think that's when more of my anxiety started.

We finally found our own home. Made it our own and ready for our little baby to arrive.

Our Son James was born in May 2001, it was an ok labour until complications arrived where I ended up having to have an emergency c-section. This meant that I needed to rely on others for support while I recovered. Now I know that grandparents want to spoil their grandchildren, but I never thought that they would take over. Recommendations are good but interfering is not what I had in mind. I know that they meant well, but at the same time, I just wanted my space back. Things didn't improve much as I ended up in hospital with a bad flu and then my heart stopped beating for a short while. I was in intensive care for 5 days on a monitor, luckily, I have made it through and have had a second chance in life. Well, that's what I thought …

Fast forward 10 years, my anxiety got worse, fear of failure, and OCD started.

As mentioned earlier, grandparents can be loving but also very controlling. I often felt that they always wanted to do one better than us by giving more to our son than what we could afford. I remember one Christmas we struggled a little financially, instead of supporting us, they told our son that he should not expect much of us that year. Now who says that to a young child? I was so angry but still was not able to speak up. All I could do was to reassure our son, that all is well, and that he will have a lovely Christmas. I was trying to teach him that money is not everything and that what counts is the love that we have for each other, food on the table, and lots of fun and laughter.

I need not have worried; he did have a lovely Christmas, I managed to get hold of a gift that he had been wanting and it made me smile to see his face with excitement. My in-laws were not so impressed, questioning us about where we got the money from. All his birthdays and Christmas gifts off them had always been 2 fifty-pound notes that he could spend on whatever he wanted. Again, I don't mind that, but when they know that we can't always afford that much I found it a little intimidating. This continued throughout our sons' teenage years.

I had no problem with James going to see his grandparents after school for his regular tea and biscuits. Maybe I was a little bit jealous of their relationship with him.

Although I always thought that I had a good relationship with James, we were both very stubborn, wanting to be right and then arguments would start. A typical teenager I got told, yes maybe, but it was hard for me as I wanted to keep a good relationship with him. I wanted to be someone he could turn to and trust as I did not get that opportunity with my mum. You know what they say, 'You always try and bring up your children differently to how your parents brought you up', it may not be for everyone but that is certainly what I wanted. As a typical teenager, when I spoke to him, I just get a grunt or 'Yeah but they don't teach us that in school' when we asked him to do some chores or to start saving his money.

One day after I got back home from work, I got told by my husband that James had got his bag and left. I was so confused and did not understand why.

They had a little conversation earlier that day, that James needs to start pulling his weight a bit more and show us a bit of respect. We have never asked much of him, just the usual kind of things like, keeping your room tidy, taking your dishes down, emptying the bin and dishwasher. As parents, we work hard to keep a roof over our heads, pay the bills, and provide food on the table. We do our very best don't we, so asking for a little bit of help wasn't much was it?

He was not happy as his dad said that buying a car for him would be on hold until he can show us some responsibility. That's only fair right?

Well, he got his own way, moved in with his grandparents, and never looked back and to this day we have lost all communication with him. And yes, you guessed it he got everything given to him by his grandparents, including the car.

This is what sent me over the edge, I was so paranoid, thinking I'm not good enough, and my eating disorder started again – saying things are not cooked, I lost a lot of weight and sank into depression.

I had been honest about everything to my work colleagues, I thought that they would support me, instead, I felt judged and bullied out of my senior role. This is what made me silence my voice.

I was overthinking the worst-case scenarios, it kept me up at night, crying my eyes out. OCD took its toll on me, even just driving a car I had to retrace my tracks, thinking I'd hit something. It was a horrible place to be stuck in. Checking everything is turned off, and taking photos as evidence, I just lost control. I lost who I was. I felt that I could not talk to anyone in case I get judged or hurt.

It is true what they say, 'you hit rock bottom before you find yourself again'. I got so low and depressed that I got put on antidepressants. Yes, they work, but I also had to work on my mindset. I found meditation, journal writing, and crystals helped me get through my worst. One thing I have become to realise, I have lived and held onto my past. Not wanting to let go and that I had been afraid of failure for far too long.

'Feel the fear and do it anyway'.

I managed to work on myself, find myself again and what it was I wanted to do. I have now set up my own clinic as a Complementary therapist and help others physically, mentally, and emotionally with my therapies.

Darren has been my biggest support; I love him so much and I am grateful for every day we have. To this day I still have no contact with our son, but I am hopeful that one day he will find us again.

Memories from the kitchen

Pasta Salad

This dish brings back memories from my childhood and is still my all-time favourite.

It is one that I have continued to use and shared with my own family. It is a quick dish, maybe not for everyone as you add vegetables and fruit to it, but you can also add your own ingredients to it.

Traditionally this is great for the summer, ideal for picnics or BBQs.

Ingredients

Cooked pasta (pasta amount depends on how much you want to make)
Tin of peas and carrots or add your own homegrown veg to it
Tin of mandarin pieces
Mayo
Salt and pepper

The method is so simple – add all ingredients together in a dish, mayo is dependent on flavour, mix it all together and boom there is your quick simple pasta dish ready in minutes.

This will keep in the fridge for a couple of days.

Bratkartoffeln (fried potatoes)

Another childhood favourite of mine and one that my husband enjoys too. Also, a quick and simple recipe.

Ingredients
4 or 5 potatoes
1 onion
2 or 3 eggs
Salt and pepper

Method – quick and simple

Peel potatoes and then cut into slices – par boil for 5 mins on high/med heat
Drain well
Cut onion into small slices
1 tbsp oil into a frying pan
Start frying the onions
Add potatoes and fry until lightly browned – may need to add more oil as you got to stop it from sticking to your pan
Once ready add all 3 eggs to the frying pan and mix it all in (I usually do this for the last 4/5 min)
Add salt and pepper to flavour and serve

I add apple sauce to mine (a memory from my grandma's and mum's kitchen) as a little side but can be eaten on its own.
Enjoy

If you would like to learn more about holistic health and wellbeing, you can connect with Jackie here:

Holistic Health and Wellbeing with Jackie
https://www.facebook.com/groups/228548571767459/

Smile and shine
Jackie xx

LISA WILLIAMS

Lisa is a multi-passionate entrepreneur dedicated to guiding and uplifting others on their spiritual journeys as a Spiritual Empowerment Mentor, Founder of Spiritual Sisters Collective, Dance Teacher & Podcast host at Raw & Real with Lisa Williams.

Lisa believes in the power of movement as a means of expression, healing, and personal growth. Through dance, she encourages others to tap into their creativity and embody their emotions freely. Lisa's journey has been guided by her own experiences, challenges, and self-discovery. She wholeheartedly believes that everyone has the potential to transform their lives and discover their inner light. Her story is her inspiration for her continued work and dedication.

Have you ever been told you're too sensitive, too loud, too bold, too weird, or too anything? Well, I have most of my life. It was something that happened no matter who I was around whether family or school peers, or even at the start of my business and entrepreneur journey when I was told I was way too kind to be successful. I mean, how the fuck can anyone be too kind? This is something that has affected me most of my life. It's like the more people told me this the more it sank deeper and deeper into my subconscious.

I had a very strange and violent upbringing. We had this very beautiful big unfinished old house. But we didn't live in much of it. My days were filled with a mixture of loneliness, quietness, loud shouting, anger, rage, and violence which all became the norm. But I knew deep down there was nothing normal about it.

Every day this beautiful little girl with a heart full of wonder and imagination would often daydream of the possibilities to have a picture-perfect home and family. One where she felt safe, where laughter was a natural part of each day. Where her Dad was a superhero like the ones you see in movies and her Mum was happy and content cooking and baking. Where they could have a fluffy cuddly dog called Benji to complete their happy home. It truly was my fairytale.

It would be a safe space where I would be able to speak without worrying about the consequences. Unfortunately, life was more of a nightmare that crept into other areas of my life, school, college, and work. Always feeling the odd one out, the one that was too anything to fit in.

Although I could delve much deeper into the pain of my past, I know that when the time is right lots of truths will come out. But for now, what I will say is that my childhood and young adult life have given me so much more empathy for others.

I have always had the gift of reading other people's energies and intentions. I did block my intuitive knowing for almost a decade but now she's back and she has risen once again like a Phoenix with so much passion to give other women the confidence to unlock and unleash their voices. As a Spiritual Empowerment Mentor & Podcaster giving other women a platform to feel seen, heard, and supported through a safe and sacred space and a place to share their knowledge and wisdom I have stepped into my gifts and power.

And talking of safe spaces and wisdom I want to introduce you to someone who loved, cared, and inspired me to be the person I am today.

My beautiful Nanny Peggy!

She was a shy and loving soul, standing at just 5 feet tall but an absolute force to be reckoned with in the kitchen spending most of her life cooking and baking and creating Kitchen Magic. She filled her home with beautiful scents and smells of joy. She loved nothing more than feeding her family delicious homemade food and filling our bellies. But the memories she created will fill our hearts forever. And I feel such gratitude to have the honour to share with you some of the stories and memories I have with her in the kitchen and beyond.

I spent most of my childhood moving back and forth with my grandparents with the food being the heart of the family home. This house was always filled with love and kindness. This place I could be anything I wanted to be, a stark difference from the house I shared with my mum and dad. Here the music would be on the wireless, that's what they called the radio, playing 1940s songs like Glenn Miller In The Mood that filled this big old and freezing cold house with so much warmth.

I was always totally mesmerised. By the way that my Nanny Peggy would start with just a few simple ingredients and turn them into something magnificent. I never knew we didn't have much money because my belly would always be full, and singing and laughter were always so present. From savoury and sweet pies, Welsh cakes, homemade chips, eggy bread, and soups to amazing Sunday roasts. So many delights to fill our bellies and souls.

One of my many favourite creations that My Nanny Peggy used to make was an apple pie. And if I sit quietly, I can take myself right back to being with her, I can smell the inviting sweet smells of the stewed cooking apples. Delicious memories! My Nanny Peggy would give me the important duty of stirring them to perfection and showing me that kitchen magic is all about the love and intention you give it. I remember the way that the sugar would sparkle and glitter and once the stewed apples were cooked to perfection, she would let it cool slightly, and at this time she would make something that I would say would go on to be a Nanny Peggy legacy. Her intricate pastry leaves. These leaves would be the finishing touch of her delicious apple pie. She would give me some of the leftover pastry and as I mindfully felt the flour between my small hands with so much excitement, I went on to try and create her eye-catching leaves. The in-depth way she would carve out the leaves and the pattern were the most wonderful thing I have ever seen. And even to this day, as I try to create these awesome pastry leaves they will never be quite like Nanny Peggy's but all the same I feel her with me in these moments.

At the time, I didn't know how prominent these memories would be, the wisdom, knowledge, kindness, and compassion that would lead me to where I am today.

On the weekend, extended family and friends would visit and one of the things that myself and my cousins absolutely loved our Nan to do was homemade chips. In a foil cone. Nanny Peggy would say "Roll Up, Roll Up, Get Your Chips in a Cone Here" We would form a queue and pretend to give her money. My Grampy would be ready with the salt and vinegar. The sheer comfort of these gorgeous homemade chips wrapped in the love of her handmade foil cones. I just remember feeling truly rich and so happy.

The truth is baking with My Nanny Peggy or watching her cook was not just about following recipes. It was about the lessons themselves. She taught me the importance of patience; reminded me that good things come to those who wait whether that was a slow simmering of a sauce or a gentle kneading of a dough. Now I emphasise the value of taking time and allowing things to develop in their natural time. Those moments have not just taught me to savour food but the journey. Teaching me about love, resilience, and the power of tradition.

What I love about these memories is recreating them with my daughter, sharing experiences that can be passed on from generation to generation. The way that a sweet smell will take you back to that beautiful moment. Knowing that at any time that I want my Nanny Peggy to be with me, I can create that not just through visualisation or intention of her visiting me as my spirit guide but, through the smells of spices and the creations that she made. For that, I'm forever grateful.

Food Memory

I want to share with you a memory and moment that is one of my most cherished. Called tomato soup and thunder.

My Mum was a waitress so worked most evenings, so I begged her on this particular night to stay over at my grandparents. It was one of many nights that I could sense my Dad's anger and I really didn't want to be around him, not that I ever did, to be honest. My Mum agreed but we didn't have much time to get there because she was due to start her shift. So, I quickly grabbed my teddy which was a dog called Sandy, and a nightie, and off we went. As we arrived My Grampy was just leaving for a night out all dressed up in a navy suit looking very handsome he gave me a kiss and off he went. My Mum, as always rushing and anxious, shouted "See you tomorrow" Nanny was standing in her cozy kitchen, with a symphony of aromas dancing through the air. Her skilled small gentle hands delicately handled the vibrant red tomatoes, preparing each ingredient with unwavering love and precision. The rich aroma of simmering herbs and spices made my mouth water with promises of warmth and comfort. With every stir of the spoon, the soup transformed into, as always, a masterpiece. Each spoonful was a burst of flavours that came together in perfect harmony. The tomato soup was radiating, offering a velvety texture that was simply divine. It was a bowl of pure bliss, brimming with the essence of homemade goodness, and a testament to my Nan's unwavering dedication to creating the most beautiful and satisfying food for the soul.

All of a sudden we heard a loud bang we both jumped out of our skin and everything went dark. The loud bang was thunder that literally felt like it shook this big old house. Nanny searched for My Grampy's heavy torch. As we huddled together, seeking solace in each other's presence, the storm raged on outside. The thunder roared once more, shaking the house with such intensity that we could feel the vibrations under our feet. It was as if the elements were engaging in a musical of chaos, reminding us of our insignificance in the face of nature's immense power. And as the storm grew more and more shaking our single-glazed windows, the rain came down in bucket loads hitting and crashing against the windows, the thunder was relentless and the lightning bolts were like disco lights. And yet at this moment, I felt a complete sense of comfort.

My Nan wrapped me in a woollen blanket, and we cuddled and ate the beautiful homemade soup. Despite the intensity of the storm, the warmth of the soup and the love of my Nan brought me such peace. And as we cuddled and ate our soup, we embraced the storm. This taught me many lessons. This is a reminder for us all:

That even in our darkest, stormiest times, there is always time for cuddles and soup.

I could share so many of Nanny Peggy's Recipes.
But my absolute favourite to make with her and of course eat too was her Welsh cakes.
Not only is this my favourite but also my welsh Heritage.

Recipe

Nanny Peggy's Traditional Welsh Cake

Ingredients:

- 225g self-raising flour
- 115g unsalted butter (diced) back in the day my nanny would occasionally use lard.
- 75g caster sugar
- 50g currants or raisins
- 1/2 teaspoon mixed spice
- 1/4 teaspoon ground cinnamon
- A pinch of salt
- 1 large egg (beaten) Add an additional egg if you need to.
- A splash of milk
- Extra butter for greasing

Instructions & Fun.

- In a mixing bowl, sift the flour, mixed spice, cinnamon, and salt together. Add the diced butter and rub it into the flour mixture using your fingertips until it resembles breadcrumbs.
- Stir in the sugar and currants (or raisins) into the mixture.
- Make a well in the centre and add the beaten egg. Mix it in with a spoon, gradually incorporating the flour mixture.
- If the mixture seems dry, add a splash of milk (or an additional egg) to bring it together into a soft dough. Avoid over-mixing; just combine until the dough is formed.

- Lightly flour a clean surface and roll out the dough to a thickness of about 5mm (1/4 inch). Use a round cookie cutter to cut out individual cakes.
- Grease a griddle or a frying pan with a little butter and place it over medium heat. Cook the Welsh cakes in batches, for about 2-3 minutes on each side, or until they turn golden brown.
- Transfer the cooked Welsh cakes onto a wire rack to cool.
- Sprinkle with a little extra caster sugar while they are still warm.
- Serve the Welsh cakes warm or at room temperature, with a lovely cup of your favourite warm drink.

Enjoy your homemade traditional Nanny Peggy's Welsh Cakes!

You can continue to be in my world and follow my journey by connecting with me at
https://spiritualsisterscollective.vipmembervault.com

And Raw & Real With Lisa Williams
https://rawrealwithlisawilliams.buzzsprout.com/

The Light within me can see and celebrates the Light within you.

Lisa x

KALLIA PAPADOPOULOS

Kallia, a passionate book blogger, a love for books that have no bounds and has an ever-growing collection of reviews. Kallia's blog is a haven where you'll discover fresh perspectives, and honest opinions, about the written word. So, if you crave literary delights and seek a guide who shares your passion for books, follow her blog to embark on a great reading journey.

"I have been reading for as long as I can remember and it has given me so much joy. It has helped in tough times and has had a positive impact on my mental health."

Kallia lives in Essex with her partner and is currently taking the book world by storm.

FESTIVE FEELINGS

I woke up knowing it was going to be an incredible day. That happy feeling crept up to my face and into my heart. It was Christmas Day! The magical wonder had culminated and today was the day! The excitement had been brewing and I just felt like a Jack in a box; I couldn't contain the buzz in me. I leaped down the stairs and made it known that I was excited, everyone was just looking at me. It was then the familiar disempowering words began.

"Kallia, sit still".

"I can't please let's go."

"We will go at 2pm"

"Oh, let's go now."

"No, you'll have to wait."

"I don't want to."

I kept looking at the clock wanting it to speed up, but it wouldn't. I was getting annoyed, tapping my fingers and I just couldn't sit still much to the annoyance of my mum and family.

Anyway, the time had arrived, and we set off! We were going to spend the day with my beloved Aunty Georgia. Such a special lady and every Christmas spent with her was an absolute joy; she only lived on the next road to us. So, as we approached her door and rang the doorbell, I was jumping up and down. I couldn't stop. I was like a puppy and wanted to run straight in! When we entered her house, the smell of her cooking just hit me. I will always remember how that made me feel; warm and loved. A feeling that remains with me to this day. Even now, as I reflect upon that cherished memory, waiting to be greeted and the feelings it evokes are still there in my mind. The warmth has become part of my being, leaving an everlasting memory on my soul. It serves as a reminder of the power of family and love. Anyway, daydreaming over back to the day:

I then had to make a dash to the kitchen to see all the food on display. The food is on the counter. My god, there's so much. Oooh happy days!! Every Christmas. The same food. So much. I want it all. The excitement is the same every single year; I'm just in awe of how Aunty can have the energy to prepare it all and smile. Smile because preparing all this food must be stressful. I wanted to eat all the food on offer and of course save some space, as I do every year, for my Aunty Georgia's cherry cheesecake. It is the best in the world. I have told everyone this. I can't stop staring and staring again. The food is fit for a king. I just feel so spoilt. Aunty makes us all feel special and I love being with her every day. But Christmas is more special because of her. Every year, there are so many people here. I just love it. Everyone is happy. I'm happy. At least for one day, everyone has something to be thankful for. People chatting away and getting ready for our feast. Each year the same people get together and celebrate; I genuinely love this and I think about it all the time.

Aunty is in the kitchen. She's smiling and has her apron on. My mum doesn't help as she doesn't like cooking. I love my Aunty. She helps me. She is the safe space where I can truly be myself.

Growing up my home should have been the warm and nurturing place where I felt accepted and loved, but sadly that wasn't the case. My parents found it difficult to display warmth and emotion, and it left me feeling like I wasn't loved.

But amidst my heartache, there was a shining light in my life – my aunt. She became my safe haven. From the moment I walked into her home, I felt love and acceptance from her.

With my aunt, there were no barriers to hide behind. She saw me for who I truly was and loved me unconditionally. Her home became a place where I could be myself without any judgement.

We'd spend hours talking about anything and everything. She listened to me with such patience and understanding. I could feel that she cared about me.

Her love was a lifeline. It gave me the strength to face the challenges at home and beyond.

Even though I found comfort in my aunt's love, the yearning for acceptance from my parents never disappeared. I couldn't help but wonder why I didn't feel that same warmth in my own home.

Throughout this rollercoaster of emotions, my aunt stood by my side.

In the end, I came to realise that home isn't just a physical place; it's a feeling. It's that sense of belonging and love that you find in the people who care about you. And for me, that home was in the arms of my aunt. It was my aunty that took me to Greek school. The food she cooked was so great, I even remember trying to get extra dinner by telling her my mum hadn't fed me. I just love food. Christmas with her is just the best so let's return to that Christmas day.

The games have started in the living room. Monopoly on the floor. About ten of us. All cheating. Same every year. I love it though. I feel wanted and loved. I feel happy. Not alone. Then I think about when I will be going home and for just a moment the loneliness and self-doubt creeps in. But, no! For now, let's play. Shouts of "Kallia, come on. Your turn!" "I want cheesecake," "Who wants cheesecake?" bring me back to the here and now. In the midst of the festive games and laughter, my mind couldn't help but wander to the delightful cherry cheesecake that awaited us in the kitchen. The mere thought of its velvety texture and the burst of sweet, tangy flavour sent my taste buds into a frenzy. I glanced around at my family members, and their eager expressions mirrored my own anticipation. Who could resist such a heavenly creation? Of course, we all want cheesecake. We run to the kitchen. As I took my first bite, the world around me faded into the background. The creamy filling danced on my tongue, complemented by the sweet tartness of the cherries. It was a harmonious symphony of flavours that enveloped my senses, evoking sheer bliss. With each subsequent bite, I savoured the impeccable balance of textures and the delightful combination of sweet and tangy notes. It was a masterpiece, a testament to Aunt Georgia's culinary skills. In between mouthfuls of the cheesecake laughter and lively conversations filled the air. We recounted stories, shared anecdotes, and embraced the joyful atmosphere of togetherness. Time seemed to stand still as we immersed ourselves in the warmth of familial bonds, cherishing every moment.

Aunt Georgia, with a heart full of love, observed our jubilant gathering from afar. Her eyes sparkled with pride and contentment, knowing that her efforts had brought happiness to each one of us. "How can you cook so well?" I couldn't help but ask, my admiration overflowing. Aunt Georgia's response was humble and heartfelt. "It's nothing special, my dear. I cook because it brings joy to everyone's hearts." Her words resonated within me, reminding me of the incredible power of food to nourish not just our bodies but also our souls. It was her love and selflessness that infused every dish she prepared, making each bite a celebration of love, family, and cherished memories. I'm fit to burst both in love and filled with food.

After eating the dreamy cheesecake, we returned to playing Monopoly. The sense of belonging and just being amongst family filled me with joy. I wish I could have this all day every day. Then again if I did, would I love it as much? Returning to the ongoing game of Monopoly, I immersed myself in the playful banter and friendly competition. It didn't matter that we bickered occasionally; it was all part of the dynamic we shared as cousins. We were as thick as thieves. Our bond continues and will do, and even though we don't see each other often, those early memories have remained with me. They serve as a reminder of how keeping hold of such special times helps us. It helps us to understand even though we may drift apart, and don't connect as often, that our love is ever-present.

As the day unfolded, laughter filled the air, intermingled with the aroma of Christmas delights and the sounds of joyful conversation. There was an inexplicable sense of belonging, a feeling that this was where we were meant to be—surrounded by family, laughter, and love. In the years that followed, life took its twists and turns. As we grew older, responsibilities took hold, but I always remembered my Christmases spent with my family. During my darkest moments, when sadness and loneliness threatened to close in on me, I found comfort in the memories. I closed my eyes and transported myself back to the sights, sounds, and smells. All was well.

Black Cherry Cheesecake

Serves 10

Prep 30 minutes, plus chilling and setting

Ingredients

2 x 410g cans of black cherry 100g butter

Melted 150g digestive biscuits -crushed

1 x 11.5g sachet of lemon and lime sugar-free jelly crystals

100ml boiling water 500g extra light cream cheese

50g caster sugar

1tsp vanilla extract 150ml double cream

Method

Tip both cans of black cherry filling into a large sieve or colander placed over a bowl and leave to drain off some of the sauce.

Mix the melted butter and biscuit crumbs together. Tip them into a 20cm (8 inch) loose-based cake tin or deep flan dish and press in an even layer over the base. Chill for at least 20 minutes.

Put the jelly crystals into a measuring jug and add the boiling water, then leave for 2-3 minutes, stirring occasionally until dissolved. Cool.

Beat together the cream cheese, caster sugar and vanilla extract. In a chilled bowl, whip the cream until it holds its shape. Fold it into the cream cheese mixture.

Pour the cooled dissolved jelly into the cream mixture, stirring gently and thoroughly. Spoon over the biscuit base and level the surface. Chill until set - about 2-3 hours.

Carefully remove the set cheesecake from the tin. Spoon the black cherry filling over

Princes 2023, *Black Cherry Cheesecake Recipe,* accessed 24 July 2023, <https://www.princes.co.uk/files/recipes/black-cherry-cheesecake-recipe.pdf>

Kallia – founder of "Books Galore"
Links:

www.booksgalore.co.uk

www.instagram.com/booksgalore77

www.twitter.com/booksgalore77

www.facebook.com/booksgaloreblog

Love to all,
Kallia

MANDY NICHOLSON

Mandy is a Creative Genius Consultant, Artist, Author, and Creative Retreat owner in Scotland and she helps creative women to launch, grow and scale their businesses and make more money.

With over 35 years of leadership and business experience, Mandy brings knowledge and wisdom to the lives of many women. However, it is her life experiences that consolidate and enhance her practical side.

Her story has become a part of her business identity and she is delighted to share a slice of it with you in this book.

THE RED THREAD

I was at rock bottom, a place I never expected to be!

In the space of twelve months, I had gone from being a senior leader with a six-figure salary and company car to a jobless single mum living in social housing. A series of traumatic and debilitating events had happened, one after the other and I had been taken from abundance to bankruptcy.

I was shaken. Stunned. Embarrassed.

However, I didn't achieve such a prestigious career without learning a thing or two. So, although what lay ahead seemed daunting, I knew I had the skills to find a way through it. What I wasn't prepared for was just how hard it was to face the uncertainty ahead alone. My first and most profound lesson was that nobody was going to come to my rescue. I truly was alone, with two children under ten and two dogs to feed. The responsibility weighed heavy on me, and I knew I couldn't let them down.

I remembered sitting with my best friend Lou just before disaster struck and holding her hand whilst she shared how unhappy she was in her marriage. We were at opposite ends of the country and unable to be together often, so I told her "There is a red thread connecting you to those people you truly love. It encircles your hearts and minds and is a symbol that you will always be there for each other despite distance, adversity, illness, or life events. It runs through the things you do and the words you say, to unite your soul's always'. It was my way of letting her know that no matter what was happening around us we would always have each other.

This message felt profound as I sat in my tiny council house contemplating how I would rebuild our lives without my children knowing we were destitute. Then something magic happened that would shine a spotlight on how important small, almost insignificant things can be. My eldest, Becca, was recounting her day at school and telling me how she had to share a precious memory about a family ritual that meant the world to her. When I asked her what she had shared she said, 'Obviously I told them that it was pancakes.'

'Pancakes'? I repeated quizzically.

'Yes, pancakes. You make the best pancakes in the world, and you taught me and Dan to make them just as good. I love making pancakes and that you never shout even when we make a mess.'

I had no idea that such a simple act had created such an impact. Becca went on to tell me that her friends were jealous because she had pancakes with maple syrup and fruit for breakfast when all they got was cereal. In fact, I had been making pancakes because they were cheap to make. It turned out that their two favourite foods were the budget recipes I had created so that they always had something good to eat without feeling poor. The red thread was there running through my actions and revealing my love for them.

A conversation about food was all the incentive I needed. The next day I made the decision to swallow my pride, accept where I was now and not where I had been, and start to rebuild our lives. We lived in an area that was a popular holiday destination, so I was going to start a cleaning business and make enough money so that my kids could keep their dance and karate lessons and never know that we were poor.

I called my mum and told her what I had planned and asked her to keep an ear open for anybody looking for cleaners. She told me she was proud of me. I was shocked. I had gone from having everything to having very little and she was still proud. When I asked her why, her answer was simple, 'You never give up Mandy, you find a solution and just do it.' I felt the red thread tugging at my heart and smiled.

Within two days I had shared my plans on social media and had signed three clients. I had a 'ducks in a row' target for how much I needed to earn to pay for everything, I hit this target within two weeks. It didn't matter that I was cleaning people's homes instead of managing a multimillion-pound business, I had purpose. Then on the Friday of the second week, my mum called to tell me there was an advert in the local paper looking for cleaners. I called and spoke to Trevor. We hit it off and thirty minutes into the call I was hired to manage his holiday cottage group located five minutes from my home. Sometimes the red thread is a line of communication filled with love. My mum knew I would never take money from her, nor charity, but in offering up a lead for me to follow, she had empowered me to change my own luck.

Cleaning became the new joy in my life. It was a job with zero responsibility, that fit around school pick-ups and I was earning more than double the minimum wage. I had decided that if I was going to be a cleaner for a while, then I would be the best damn cleaner out there. 'How you do anything is how you do everything' was my favourite saying, and I lived by it authentically. I had standards as a senior manager when I was earning such a massive salary and I applied the same standards to the work I did now, even to how I made my pancakes.

It dawned on me just how important this was, and I made an unconscious decision to weave that ethos into everything I did from that day forward. I would lay some foundations and make some money and then I would uplevel when the time was right.

We were living our best lives in our little 'castle by the sea' (my new name for my council house because it was two minutes from the beach). As a family, we would spend every day, in all weathers walking for miles with the dogs on our wonderful white sandy beaches. The kids even got up at 6 am (some mornings) to join me on the first dog walk of the day, on the understanding that we made pancakes when we returned home.

I felt aligned with the universe and was manifesting all I needed. Every penny over what was necessary was being squirrelled away into pensions and investments, one pound at a time. I was determined to create our perfect little life. We were happy.

Sometimes it is when you achieve happiness following such loss that you understand what really matters. Although my determination to rebuild bigger and better was focused, my perspective had changed. The time I had been gifted with my children through the awful events of the previous year was precious. They loved having me home and being able to take them to all their activities. I would never compromise time for wealth again. I would find a way to have both.

This became my goal. I learned to truly forgive the people who had hurt and wronged me as well as myself. I found a level of gratitude for the small things that I had never known before. My mindset changed, my attitude changed, and I became the most fulfilled and motivated I had ever been. Nothing would stop me from creating my vision.

As time passed my business evolved from a cleaning business to a financial services business organically through my new connections. The red thread was weaving a network of the right people who cared for me as I cared for them. Soon the financial services business I had built expanded into a Wills and Estate Planning business with a new partner.

Along the way, I had re-ignited a social life and had been invited to an old friend's fiftieth birthday party. I was looking and feeling great so accepted her invitation and arrived with my sister for a fun night out. I was the designated driver as I didn't drink so I was able to really enjoy the night. Thirty minutes into the evening a new guest arrived. I recognised him from my school in Berwick upon Tweed and my sister confirmed it was Gary Nicholson who had been in her year, two years younger than me.

Gary sat next to me and started chatting. As he leaned over his leg brushed against mine and it was like I just received an electric shock. We chatted all night and when I awoke the next morning, he had sent me a friend request and message on Facebook.

After a few coffee dates, Gary suggested a beach walk on a warm sunny day. As we meandered through the sand dunes he said, 'I have something to tell you'. My stomach jumped because I liked him a lot. 'I was born with cystic fibrosis and had a double lung transplant in 2004 so if we keep seeing each other I can't promise you time. I was only given six years and it's been nine, so I am living on borrowed time. I will understand if you want to cut things off now.'

I replied, 'Can I think about it and get back to you'?

When I arrived home, it felt like I had been a bit formal, and I realised I was afraid. I was falling for this man, so I needed to understand his condition. I spent the remainder of the day researching cystic fibrosis and transplants. I had to use my head and make an informed decision. But the red thread was yanking at my heart and pulling me towards this man. The next day I decided that one year of happiness beat the thirteen years of misery with my ex-husband and I went all in.

Gary moved in with us in 2014 and we were married on 16th May 2015. Life was good. My children were happy and thriving despite Dan being diagnosed with autism and Becca ADHD. My business was making money and my investments were performing exceptionally well. Then in 2016, Gary found a private house to rent round the corner from my mum and we were ready for our first uplevel.

Moving from the little house that had saved me was a wrench, but there was more space and a lovely big garden awaiting, so off we went. I continued to work hard on my business but there was a void inside me in the shape of my neglected artistic skills. I had longed to have my own successful creative business, but I believed the lies around the myth of the starving artist. One day in late 2018 Gary said, 'I am sure you could sell creative products as well as you do anything so why don't you stop talking about it and just do it'. It was the slap in the face I needed, and I embarked on a journey to find a coach who could fill in the gaps in my knowledge.

I signed up for a twelve-month program, started writing my book, and juggled all the ingredients for launching my dream business. Meanwhile, my investments were maturing, and we would be able to access them in October 2019, so we decided to buy a house for cash. We found the perfect place and all the wheels were set in motion. New business, new house, big leap.

Moving into our dream home in October 2019 as well as pressing the publish button on my book 'The Life I Won' were my third proudest moments next to having my children and marrying Gary. On boxing day of the same year, I launched my coaching business and signature program The Creative Mastermind. We had it all. But we remained humble and incredibly close as a family. Tightly bound by that red thread.

As the new year beckoned, Gary's health started to decline. Then in March 2020 as we went into lockdown, Gary went for his usual dialysis on a Tuesday morning and it would be the last time I would see him in person until 26th April, 3 days before he died. The pandemic kept me from the best man I have ever met for the last month of his life, but I remain grateful to this day for the hospital allowing me to be with him up to the moment he died at 3.40 am on 29th April 2020.

As I look back, I still feel the ups and downs deeply and I can smile and acknowledge that it's all just life's rich tapestry. We are all going to lose people. We will fail. We will experience success. Some people will appear to have more woe than others, and some will appear to have more success, but often it's an elaborate farce to elicit sympathy or envy. Nobody's life can be predicted, it is just a set of experiences, some good some bad. It is how you learn and grow that builds your character. Most importantly, it is all about that red thread connecting you to the people who mean the most.

Sometimes you need to pull the thread tight and bring people close, sometimes you need to snip it to let people go, but it will always be there in the words, actions, and physical proximity of the souls who are destined to cross your path.

Make pancakes with your children and don't spare the maple syrup. Create memories and take risks because life is too short. Love well, live well, and make a difference because the red thread continues even after you start your journey to another dimension.

I feel the pull of the thread from Gary every day and now you are part of my red thread for a moment as you finish my story.

Footnote:

Following Gary's death, after a period of grieving we invited a blind dog to join our family to heal us, his name is Beau. Then in March 2021, I decided that as Becca was going to University we would move to Scotland to fulfil my goal of owning a castle to run creative retreats from. I put the house on the market on a Monday and sold it that afternoon. The universe put a mini version of the very castle on my vision board in my path and I took the risk. I bought it, renovated it and now I run creative retreats and do B&B. I am buying the salon next door and turning it into a Bistro and Gallery, because…life is for living!

What's the worst that can happen? It already has and I survived, so bring it on.

Food Memory

From as far back as I can remember I was surrounded by post-war cooks in the form of my two grandmas'. They were feeders and there was always an abundance of food. My mum carried on this tradition of cooking and feeding, so there are so many food memories I could share. But the most significant one was my paternal grandma Cecilia King. We would visit her and Granddad George in their council house in Irlam, Manchester for a sleepover. There were treasures to be found in the bedrooms, a dressing-up cupboard under the stairs, and a sandpit in the garden, but the 'Grill Pan' was the golden goose.

My nan would grill bacon, black pudding, sausage, egg, tomato, mushrooms, and cheese all in one big grill pan so everything cooked at the same time in the bacon juices. We would sit around the table and share it and dip the juices with white bread whilst Grandad told stories about the war and his travels.

I still treasure these memories today, from both of my grandparent's houses. I can still smell the food cooking and the wet sand of the sandpit. I can still feel the excitement of finding new things to play with in the bedrooms. I can still hear my nan reading Treasure Island and The Stories of Tivvy. I can feel the faux leather sofa and coarse velvet cushions.

Food has been a significant part of the red thread woven through my life, so I want to share my greatest tradition with you.

Nicholson House Tradition

No surprises, it's pancakes!

Now that Becca is at Uni in Newcastle and we are in Scotland it is almost ceremonial when she comes to visit that we make pancakes.

It must be breakfast after her first night home and there must be fruit, maple syrup, and chocolate spread.

My kids have been known to eat nine pancakes each. Why nine? Because I always cook them in batches of three, so they fight over who goes first and alternate their batches. We even make mini dog pancakes so the whole family can enjoy them.

Guess what my recipe is going to be???

Recipe

American Style Pancakes

OK, let me start by saying I don't measure anything accurately – I feel the way.

8 heaped dessert spoons of self-raising flour
4 dessert spoons of caster sugar (more or less to taste)
1 teaspoon of baking powder
3 – 4 eggs depending on size
Milk

Add all the ingredients to a bowl and whisk well. Pour into a jug and leave to stand for 5 – 10 minutes.

The most important skill to make pancakes is the heat of your pan. I use an iron skillet and add butter then wipe it off. Test the pan heat with a small amount of batter and wait until you see bubbles appearing. Turn when the bubbles have appeared after a minute or so and cook for the same amount of time. Never fry in oil or butter, they come out best from a dry pan at the perfect heat. If it gets too dry add butter and wipe it off again.

If your pancakes are light, fluffy and rise to thick then the pan heat is good. If not, try again.

Serve with some or all - maple syrup, bananas, soft fruits, Greek yoghurt, and chocolate spread.

You can continue to be in my world by connecting with me on social media via my website: www.mandynicholson.co.uk
You can visit me in Scotland in my mini castle: www.theartbankdalbeattie.com
You can buy my book 'The Life I Won' by A J King (my pen name) and read part one of my story: https://www.amazon.co.uk/~/e/B004M41ZDG

Love & colour
Mandy

DANI LOUISE SMITH

Dani is the Queen of Business Organisation, a business coach and mentor in Leeds, West Yorkshire and she helps female entrepreneurs to empower their business, and unlock success, productivity, and profit.

With over 10 years of community building on social media, Dani brings her planning and business management system skills to service-based business women. However, it is Dani's life challenges that have contributed to her mission to empower others through education and encouragement.

Her story has become a belief she sees in so many other women and she is dedicated to sharing how you can be in charge of your own belief too.

RESILIENCE UNVEILED: FROM ENDLESS QUITTING TO UNLEASHING BELIEF

My hips swayed side to side as music played alongside laughter and the patter of my daughter's dancing feet against the kitchen floor. The energy of the room was seasoned with joy. The sizzle of the hob heated up the latest recipe my husband was trying. Dan was in his happy place, cooking and singing whilst his wife and daughter were dancing. The boys came running in, faster than lightning when their favourite song began to play. A picture-perfect family, an embodiment of pure, unconditional love.

The picture cracked, the glass shattering, fading the memory into reality. Eighteen-year-old me would never have believed that my days would be filled with so much passion and purpose, a family of five, a voice that people heard and took for gospel. A voice that back in 2011 was silent.

Before she was seen and not heard...

Lifted into the air, then rapidly falling to be captured by a human net of strong hands. Physical theatre was the only highlight of my week. The only time my body moved the way I desired and I felt free. The rest of my days were entangled in a cycle: get up, go to college, work, go to bed, and do it all over again. It was suffocating. The toxicity of a repetitive, unfulfilling cycle that my creative mind didn't want. With each passing day, my light dimmed and my happiness faded.

How can you escape if you don't know how?

I didn't desire to be an actress. I found myself following my best friend to college, setting myself up for judgement and bullying. That's exactly what followed until I spoke up and quit. Walking away with no qualifications. My first failure.

The cycle of being a quitter had begun.

Months went by of me clouding a deep depression. I lacked social connections, friends, happiness, and support from my parents, who were eager for me to get a job, move on and do something. I had gone from the 'clever clogs' daughter (I even had a keyring with this written on), whose Mum would encourage her to show off dance routines to visitors, to what felt like a disappointment. When you're considered 'clever clogs' surely, you're meant to make smart decisions?

The next 'smart move' came in the form of my passion for writing, applying for A-level English, business, and psychology. The recipe for a fresh start, right?

Upon enrolment, I was the oldest there, amongst fresh-out-of-school 16-year-olds. Alone. Quiet. Silent, again. I didn't fit in. Showing up and doing the work, I told myself it was ok, I wasn't there to make friends.
I applied for a job, but the overwhelming relationship with my boyfriend came to an end and so much was left unsaid. How much more alone could one person become?

A pinch of confidence…

You can live every day smiling, but never feel fulfilled. Have you ever felt like that? That was who I was for a short while. My first real job, 12 hours a week and blowing my wages at the weekend, my first pinch of confidence. Little did I know that every pinch of confidence would build up to the recipe for unlocking my voice.

I met my husband at that job. The cheeky chap, with huge dimples, spiked hair, and the worst chat-up lines. Little did I know how much our first date would actually change the rest of my life.

I found myself truly being me. I had opinions, I took no shit, and I was respected, appreciated, and loved. It gave me power. He probably doesn't know this, but something changed when he brought light into my life. I found something I wasn't even looking for. It's a feeling I'll never forget. Nine months into the relationship, we moved in together. I didn't want to go fast and jump in, but it felt right. I worked, we lived, we played, I was happy, fulfilled. It was enough…until two pink lines on a test confirmed pregnancy one year into the relationship. It was, of course, one of the best things to happen to me, but also something that led to my inner self being silenced.

A sprinkle of self-love…

Self-love is fundamental. I know this now. The opinions of being a young Mum ate at me. The judgement of decisions I made chewed at my confidence. The weight gain nibbled at every bit of trust in myself I had. Work life left behind, in exchange for a baby in my arms, bringing daily joy. But there was a lingering loneliness and entrapment in belonging inside a picture-perfect frame. Stay at home Mum and wife-to-be, it wasn't enough. I thrived off creativity, so I explored hobbies and found part-time work. The belief that it would help would soon spoil the broth when my manager caused anxiety. I felt watched and unable to speak through fear. I had to get out. Slowly and surely, I was becoming a shell of my former self. I found a new job and my notice went in. This new job was better. Comfortability built my confidence further, encouraging me to explore my hobbies further and start a business. It looked quite easy on social media. I gave it a go, ready to find something I could put my all into and make a success of…and I was quite good at it!

A dash of silence…

Working non-stop, a start-up business, a mum, and ready to plan a wedding. Life was moving by and yet there was still a freedom I desired. So, I quit again. First college, my A-Levels, my first job, and now my current job. I took the leap; my notice went in and I was instantly met with the fears of others,

'Oh, you'll be back. I give you four weeks!'

'I'm worried, how will you manage?'

'Why would you quit, you've got a son now?'

The cycle continued. I quit, but I listened, and I fell silent.

Excited and passionate about the possibility of being my own boss, those words haunted me. It took me right back to my 18-year-old self, when my own uncle, in front of our entire family, said that I would be a lazy stay-at-home-mum, with three kids, living off benefits. Those words haunted me so much, that is exactly who I became.

I did nothing, frozen by fear. Trapped in a cycle of procrastination. No results. A failure. This is not who I wanted to be. I was silent. My online presence was non-existent. My voice was unheard through fear of judgement of my actions. I wanted to be a success. I wanted more. Then I fell pregnant. This time was different. I was welcoming another child, so I had to take action. I started learning and I was hooked.

The baby boy arrived. The wedding was eight months away. The business was at a standstill. The baby was poorly, he didn't sleep, I didn't sleep, my husband began having knee surgeries and nothing was changing. Placed on a hamster wheel, trapped in the cycle of life, doing what I should do, and being who I should be, all whilst desiring more. I couldn't say that though. What did I have to be upset about? I was getting married, and had two beautiful boys, I should be happy. That's exactly what was said, and I was silenced. How could I possibly find light in this dark depression? How could I help my family instead of hiding away? How could I speak up and be free of this silence?

No money. No job. No hope.

The spices of life…

It gets worse before it gets better. Once you hit rock bottom, there is only one way, up! That is exactly what happened next. I was pregnant again! I may add that our last two children were planned. I know it doesn't solve much, with a husband who can reproduce but cannot work. I loved my boys so much and believed another baby would make me happier. A girl to complete our family! For a period of time, I did find myself in the baby bubble. We had married, welcomed our daughter, and used our benefits to begin saving money.

Spices ruined the stew.

My husband's disability claim was revoked, and my carers allowance was owed back, putting me into debt. We lived off our very little savings, my very little business earnings, and the food our family bought for us. There I was, a stay-at-home mum, with three kids and on benefits. How could my uncle be so right? How could previous statements be so right?

They weren't right, I was. I chose to believe and became what they said I would. It was a harsh lesson in mindset.

'Believe you can or believe you can't. You're right!'

I didn't enjoy this flavour of life. The struggle to pay bills, fight to stay out of debt, and battles to prove my husband's disability.

A simmer of light…

The consistent battle forced me to apply for a job within the NHS. I got accepted straight away. With our baby girl being six months old I wasn't comfortable going back to work whilst other mums enjoyed precious time on maternity leave. I felt I had no choice.

Christmas 2019 was when everything changed. Settled into work life, I started earning a stable income. I saw results from the business and the social aspect of working life and it really raised me up. My work family loved and supported the idea of my business. It was the confidence boost I needed. I will be forever grateful for that. As a result, I was ready to take on new opportunities.

I attended my first in-person networking meeting for Mums In Business. When I arrived, we were presented with a question.

What's one goal that you want to achieve within a year?

It was crazy that up until then I hadn't set goals. I didn't realise anything was possible. The worst part was we needed to say our goals out loud to the group. That moment was the first of many when I could say 'This is who I am, and this is what I want'. I set a goal to create my own office. Today, as I write this, I have just achieved this goal. It took longer than a year, but speaking out and saying what I wanted was just the start of unlocking my voice.

I would never have imagined that six months on we would be in a pandemic, locked down and I would be facing this killer virus on the front line. They say that the universe tests us and oh did it test my strength then.

I never felt anxiety like that before, panic attacks, high blood pressure, and palpitations. My physical and mental health, taking a hit. Unbelievably, during this time it inspired me to fight. I unleashed a fight to make a change. I put up a fight at work, speaking up to my supervisor about the management of the unpredictable situation. I put up a fight at home, speaking to my husband's doctor, as his condition worsened, demanding something was done to improve his daily challenges and quality of life. I put up a fight for myself, getting out in the world, being vulnerable but visible. I was showing up for everyone that needed me to and speaking up.

Boiling over…

Sat in that room at Christmas, a nervous wreck, I never would have imagined that a year in I would be hosting the meeting! In October 2020 I put myself forward for a networking leader position after not feeling good enough, capable, or confident. I got it! I dived into personal development, boosting my belief in myself, working on my money mindset, setting goals, and being brave enough to say them out loud.

The boiling point came when I was mastering it all, family, disabled husband, work, and business were becoming successful whilst I was bossing it with networking meetings. I was managing to organise my busy life. It felt amazing to help people from all angles.

One day a request for help with a business landed in my messages. Then another, and another. Of course, I could do that. Two members of the business community suggested I stop giving free advice and charge for it. Could I really? Did people want to hear my story? Did people want to hear how I had turned my business around? It turns out, they did!

There I was, as confident as ever, new business, making up to four jobs and three kids.

The problem with being a people pleaser is that you forget to put your oxygen mask on first and if you can't breathe, you can't help anybody else. That's exactly what I was doing and every weekend I was burning out. Sleeping the weekend away, through overwhelm, weekdays working 6am until 11pm and barely speaking to my family. I missed assemblies, didn't do school runs, and spent half term and summer breaks on a phone, laptop, or at a sewing machine. My children were growing up. Enough was enough. From inside I screamed 'Get me out!'

Chop away the fat…

I was filling my life with all things that helped others, but not feeding myself what I really wanted. I scarily cut the cord with the biggest money maker and time eater of all, the job at the hospital. I held back because of fear of judgement and fear of failure. I had to accept that this was a different vision of me now, evolved enough to say that this journey was ending and unexpectedly, those around me understood. When I accepted it myself, spoke, and announced that my notice was in, everyone else accepted it too. The power to make things happen truly comes within.

In July 2021, I worked my last shift for the NHS and stepped into a summer of fun in the sun with my family. I will never forget that feeling of freedom. I did it again, handed in my notice in November 2021 for the networking position, and stepped into that freedom. It was what I had been chasing all along.

…and now, June 2023, I sit here writing this just days after announcing the closure of my keepsakes business. An announcement I probably held for too long, as I felt like I was forgetting where I came from. The truth is, there is power in saying how you feel and making decisions based on that.

Dish the dessert…

The final taste you need to know and find comfort in is that quitting isn't a failure, instead it's stepping back from what doesn't serve you anymore.

Unlocking your voice isn't about anyone else, it's about you and your self-acceptance. Because if you truly accept your feelings and decisions, release fear and speak up from this place, you can do so as unapologetically you and others will accept that too.

Find the energy to quit when it's right to quit.

Find the energy to unlock your voice and speak up.

Your future self will thank you.

Food Memory

The kitchen was always the place family would gather, over a plate of boiled eggs and soldiers in my grandma's house, the perfect runny yolk and buttered toast. A delightful treat that I, as an adult, learned to boil to perfection, so that I could present the beautiful snack to my own children. We would go to our grandparents' house after school, myself and my sisters, where we found ourselves making a shopping list and gathering items together from the kitchen cupboards, until we were called to the round table for our meal.

My Mum would boil them at home too, alongside singing,
'Chick, chick. chick. chicken lay a little egg for me.
Chick, chick, chick, chicken I want one for my tea.'
I have to admit though, the timing skills of the boiling and cooling hadn't passed down to my Mum as nearly always they were fully boiled. Yet we still enjoyed them as they drifted us back to the memory at our grandparents' house.

These present moments over the kitchen table singing and dancing happen often in my family home now. Listening to our favourite songs whilst I boil eggs, or my husband Dan cooks traditional favourites.
I treasure those moments, where we are completely present and connected to each other, the music, the laughter, and the seasoning of the sauce on the hob. This family picture flickers, to the memories of Grandma buttering the toast, my Mum singing her chucky egg song and back to us moving to the music together, at home, in the kitchen.

Grandparents' House Tradition

Ok, it's a simple one, because I am no master chef myself, but so many people rarely hit the spot with their runny 'eggs and soldiers'.

So, I am going to teach you how to make them perfectly, my grandma's way, and the way that my younger two children love to splash their toast into and a lot of the time pinch mine before I am about to sit down and eat it.

Back at Grandma's kitchen table, we had plenty of eggs to go around, with a huge plate of toast to share in the middle and a fight to get the last 'soldier' to dip, after helping each other to crack the head and take off the 'helmet' on the egg.

To this day, I could sit and peel boiled eggs for hours, I love it. Peel it perfectly smooth, ready to dig your spoon into, whilst it's still warm but cool enough to have slowed down cooking.

Here is how to get yours just right…

Recipe

Chucky Eggs and Soldiers

As many eggs as you desire, I love to have three!
Two slices of bread. I find four or five soldiers to one egg works best!
A full kettle of boiling water
Butter

Set your timer to six minutes.

Boil a full kettle of water and add a pan with eggs inside to the hob.

Pour in the boiling water, taking care not to pour directly onto eggs as they will crack.

Turn the heat up to full and press start on your timer.

Put your slices of toast in for two minutes. (Or as desired)

Lather toast with loads of butter, so that it soaks in nicely. My husband says that my toast is 'warm bread', perfect for dipping!

Once the timer goes off, empty the hot water into the kitchen sink.
Turn on the cold tap to full and run your boiled eggs under cold water for 5 minutes.

Slice buttered toast in half. Then Slice each half into four 'strips' to create your soldiers.

Drain water from eggs, place on egg cups beside your soldiers, and enjoy!

The most important part of creating the yummy yolk is to ensure you stick to the times precisely, getting the eggs under that cold water almost instantly, otherwise, they continue to cook, and you have solid, boiled eggs.

If your eggs are coming out overcooked, ensure you turn up the heat and pour in the boiling water at almost the same time, and don't waste a second before you hit the timer.
Serve for breakfast or a midday snack and enjoy!

You can discover your inner Queen of Organisation, over on my social media communities @queenofbusinessorganisation,

Access useful business resources via my website at;
www.queenofbusinessorganisation.co.uk

You can buy my masterclasses, courses, and templates at
https://www.etsy.com/uk/shop/Queenoforganisation

All the best,
Dani

EL JEDRAS

El Jedras is a visionary leader, making waves as the CEO of Evolveology® and Feminology UK Retreats. With an innate gift as an Intuitive Psychic, El guides individuals on transformative journeys of personal and business growth, helping them unlock their true potential.

El is a gifted author with two best-selling books to her name. Her written words inspire and empower readers to embrace their power and find success and happiness. With an unshakable passion for witnessing people evolve into their most powerful, successful, and happiest versions, El Jedras continues to make a positive impact in both the personal and professional spheres, leaving a trail of inspiration and transformation wherever she goes.

Silenced by Those That Loved Me

How could they have loved me that much but silenced my voice when I needed to be heard the most? This question lives within me, flowing through my entire being, constantly reminding me of their love and their suppression. This is my story—a narrative of my dreams and my voice being muted and the unyielding pursuit to find my voice amidst the resounding silence.

One of my earliest memories takes me back to the tiny cups of coffee. I recall the pride I felt as I served it to guests in our home, carefully balancing a tray adorned with the vibrant red and white Turkish flag. The delicate porcelain cups, decorated with dainty yellow and pink flowers, held a timeless charm. It seemed almost customary in our Turkish Cypriot community for each household to possess these cups. Even at the tender age of 7 or 8, I eagerly lent a hand in carrying the tray, the aroma of freshly roasted coffee wafting through the air, filling the cups to the brim. The coffee, brewed with a unique intensity, carried notes of roasted, almost burnt spices, a hint of bitterness intertwined with an earthy tobacco essence. Alongside, we placed matching petite plates, completing the presentation. It was a tradition that involved offering glasses of water on the side, though reserved exclusively for the men in attendance.

Men would swiftly drink their coffee and move on to the water, while women engaged in a fascinating ritual. After savouring their coffee, women would carefully turn their cups upside down, tilting them in various draining positions, and then finally turning them upright to reveal the powdery residue etched across the cup's interior. These intricate markings held deep meaning. They were not merely coffee remnants, but rather a language of symbols and messages waiting to be deciphered. This sacred art of coffee cup reading was an exclusive practice among women, a tradition passed down through generations. I was always intrigued, yearning to explore this hidden world for myself. However, whenever I expressed my curiosity and eagerness to learn, I was met with dismissive responses, being told it wasn't meant for me and to simply move along.

It wasn't until I reached the age of around 12 that I finally had the opportunity to learn the art of preparing the perfect Turkish coffee. It was a significant milestone, a rite of passage for a young girl to comprehend the intricacies of taking orders from family and guests and preparing the coffee just the way they preferred it. Whether it was with or without crema, with a touch of sugar, or enjoyed plain, mastering the technique became a cherished skill. It symbolized not only my growing independence but also my ability to contribute and serve within our household.

From a tender age, my role in life was unmistakably clear — I existed to serve. It was ingrained in me that my purpose was to cater to others: the men, the elders, and the needs of my household. I was expected to blend in seamlessly, adhering to the prescribed behaviours of a "good girl." Everything from how I spoke, dressed, ate, and even sat was meticulously regulated. Growing up in a deeply traditional Turkish Cypriot family, certain ideals were instilled in us as girls. We were taught that our ultimate destiny was to be married as virgins, with arranged marriages lurking as a distinct possibility. I often heard stories from my elders, recounting wedding nights and the anticipation of a white sheet prepared to confirm the consummation through the presence of a virgin bride's blood. These stories, absorbed into my young mind, began to shape my future reality.

I grew up wholeheartedly believing that honouring my family and conforming to my parent's expectations was the only path to follow. I obediently embraced these beliefs until a pivotal moment when I was nine years old: the birth of my younger brother, our family's first son. It was a joyous occasion for all of us, as my sisters and I welcomed another sibling into our lives. However, as our family dynamic evolved, I began to witness a shift in how we were treated based on our genders. Gradually, I noticed that my brother, simply by virtue of being a boy, was granted certain privileges that were denied to us. He was allowed to stay up later than we were, enjoy outings with our father on Sundays, join football clubs, and even occupy the coveted front seat in the car. I couldn't help but overhear phrases like "he's a boy, that's why..." and "Yes, he can because he's a boy." I couldn't fully comprehend or accept the messages I was receiving, but they somehow aligned with the narrative that had been ingrained in me since childhood: that girls were considered secondary. Despite my love for my brother, I struggled to digest this reality, which seemed to reinforce the notion of my own inferiority.

Countless fleeting moments slipped away from me, as I remained silent, bound by the expectations placed upon me as a child. I understood my role and knew I was meant to stay quiet, to never make waves or disrupt the established order. While my family loved me unquestionably, this pattern of silence and submission persisted through the generations, as it had always been.

A shift started to occur within me as I became increasingly self-aware. It was as if a young age awakening was taking place, unfolding my consciousness to the world around me. By the time I reached the age of around 10, I had spent years absorbing, listening, and internalising everything and everyone around me. However, this awakening brought forth my own voice and beliefs, which began to clash with the narratives I had absorbed.

Despite this inner turmoil, I remained silent, sensing that something was brewing beneath the surface. Deep inside, I knew that certain things no longer felt right, even though I struggled to articulate them at the time.

I reflect on my journey of self-discovery, unsure of when my awareness of my feminine body first emerged. Looking back, I know it was during my tender years. Surrounded by my teddies in bed, I contemplated my body and the sensations I experienced. Some moments brought pleasure, while others stirred an unsettling and unfamiliar feeling within my chest, I now know this feeling to be one of shame and guilt.

The rule I was to live by loomed over me: the rule of remaining a virgin. Yet, its true meaning eluded my young understanding. Innocence intertwined with curiosity, beckoning me to explore what was offered to me as a gift from someone close. I failed to grasp the distinction between play and reality, and for years, it all seemed like an innocent surrender to what children did. However, my curiosity blurred the boundaries, breaching the realm of what should be confined to childhood play.

Years passed before I gained enough courage to share this reality with my mother. But the closeness of our connection stifled the conversation. Tears fell, only to be wiped away, never to be mentioned again. It was in that pivotal moment that I realized, for the first time, that those who professed love were silencing me. The painful truth washed over me—I was being silenced by those who claimed to love me.

I recall a particular day whilst on holiday in North Cyprus, as I often visited during the peak of summer. It was August when his grandmother invited me to her home, which I soon realised was an opportunity to escape the watchful eyes and ears of our families, a chance for us to connect. She beckoned me into her modest, half-manufactured kitchen and offered me Turkish coffee, something I had only recently been allowed to try at the age of 17. I agreed to have the coffee and opted for sugar, believing it would help counterbalance the bitterness of the espresso-like brew.

At that moment, I sensed his arrival alongside his mother, and his grandmother declared that she needed to speak with her, leaving us alone in the tiny kitchen. Her parting words were to prepare coffee for all of us. I quickly surveyed the ingredients and tools neatly arranged, realising I would be tasked with making coffee for everyone, including the man I thought would be my future husband.

With a smile, I greeted him, instantly captivated by a familiar scent—one I had come to love. Though we had only crossed paths a few times within our families, I instinctively felt drawn to that intoxicating aroma, which ignited waves of emotion and excitement within me. As I began the process of making coffee, we exchanged customary pleasantries, but his eagerness to be near me became evident. Before I could even complete the coffee-making ritual, I felt his hands on my waist from behind as he moved close to my body. The scent of his presence mingled with the rich aroma of coffee, etching a memory that I could still conjure by simply closing my eyes. However, it is no longer a moment of passion and anticipation; instead, it serves as a reminder of a stirring within my body that I wish to forget.

What I initially perceived as my parents' aspirations for me, and at that point in time, I genuinely believed it might be the destined path for my story, ultimately revealed itself as a continuation of my pattern: a cycle of seeking love, only to be met with pain.

.

He, too, inflicted deep wounds upon me, causing immense emotional pain and confusion within my mind and body. It happened after just one date, the first time we went out together with my parent's consent. I left feeling like I was so grown up being allowed to be with a man with my parent's consent, a man I hoped to marry to complete the traditions my family wanted for me. But it wasn't the romantic date I had hoped for and as he dropped me off at home, he wore an innocent smile on his face, while I masked the turmoil within. In my naivety, I believed he loved me, only to discover that once again, someone I cherished had shattered the boundaries of my silence. And to this day, that silence remains unbroken.

At the age of 22, I believed I had already learned many valuable lessons in life. However, experiencing love in the right way was still on my journey of discovery. Then, I met someone who felt different, someone with whom I shared a unique connection I had never felt before. My instincts told me that perhaps this person was my match, the one who would change my future and truly listen to me. Unfortunately, the toxicity gradually seeped into our relationship, and I found myself trapped in an eight-year cycle of never-ending darkness. I held onto hope, yearning for our success, but each time I believed he truly understood and embraced me, he would let me down, leaving yet another scar on my already fragile soul.

The pain he left in his wake served as a catalyst, reigniting the dormant emotions within me. It was then that I came to a profound realisation – to truly love, one must embrace the power of allowing voices to be heard.

To ensure that I didn't fall back into the familiar cycle I had been trapped in, I made the brave decision to leave behind everything I knew, including a toxic relationship. It meant creating distance not only from my previous life with him but also from my job, my city, and my friends. It was a necessary and transformative step to break free from the constraints that held me captive and start afresh. By forging a new path, I aimed to liberate myself from his grasp and open myself up to the boundless possibilities of growth, healing, and creating a life that truly honoured my voice. It was a journey of empowerment, where I embraced authenticity and reclaimed my right to live on my own terms for the first time.

What emerged during that pivotal period was an extraordinary force, unlike anything I had ever experienced or learned. It was the resounding echo of my own voice, reverberating with a power that could not be denied. No longer willing to be silenced, I understood that to break the patterns of the future, my voice must be heard. It became the singular element of strength I had longed for, and when I discovered it, my life transformed in wondrous, enchanting ways. It was a magnificent awakening, an awe-inspiring journey of self-realization and empowerment.

I want to wrap up this story on a positive note, as it is what we have all come to anticipate. I am incredibly grateful to share the happy ending of my journey with all of you in this chapter. Along the way, I met a man who became my hero. Now, I have the joy of raising three beautiful children I call them my three little heroes.

In addition, I am honoured to serve as the CEO of my own company, 'Evolveology,' where I wholeheartedly dedicate myself to supporting women on their healing journeys. With utmost compassion, I guide them in overcoming the wounds inflicted from their past, empowering them to reclaim their voices and create their own profound happiness. Together, we embark on a transformative path of resilience, growth, and self-discovery, fostering a community where wounds can heal, and authentic joy can flourish.

I realised that merely dreaming of a perfect life served no purpose, I had to take action and create it myself. Setting boundaries became imperative, and using my voice became essential to ensure that I was heard. Rebuilding trust began with me, laying a solid foundation before extending it to others. I embarked on a journey to discover how I wanted to be loved, recognising that true love flourished only when I learned to love myself. Relearning intimacy meant embracing pleasure and trust, casting aside the shackles of fear. The process involved healing from the persistent burden of shame and guilt that had permeated every cell of my being.

And so, I did. I share this story as a testament that I am but one among many. No longer silenced by those who love me, I discovered the power within to heal and evolve. You, too, possess this remarkable power. While your past may reside within your subconscious mind, it is your conscious mind that holds the true ability to shape your future. Choose to free yourself from the shackles of silence and embrace your voice.

Choose the path of growth and transformation.

Choose love and happiness above all else, for you have the capacity to do so. Together, we can evolve and thrive.

Making Turkish Coffee

Making Turkish Coffee, also known as Turkish coffee or Türk Kahvesi, is a traditional method of preparing coffee that has been popular in Turkey, Northern Cyprus, and the surrounding regions for centuries. It's a strong, rich, and flavorful coffee served in small cups without milk. Here's the art of making Turkish coffee:

Ingredients

Freshly ground coffee beans (Turkish coffee grind, finer than espresso grind)
Cold water
Sugar (optional)
Turkish coffee pot (cezve/ibrik)
Small cups for serving and a small spoon for stirring

Instructions

1. Measure the ingredients: The standard measurement for one cup of Turkish coffee is one cup of water (approximately 75 ml) and one heaping teaspoon of coffee per serving. You can add sugar based on your preference for sweetness.

2. Add water and sugar (optional): Pour the cold water into the Turkish coffee pot (cezve/ibrik) and add sugar to taste if you prefer your coffee sweet. Stir the mixture gently until the sugar is dissolved. And then add the heaping teaspoon of finely ground coffee to the pot for each serving. Do not stir at this point.

3. Heat the coffee: Place the Turkish coffee pot on low heat. It's essential to use low heat to give the flavors time to develop without boiling the coffee rapidly. Slow heating is a crucial aspect of making Turkish coffee.

4. Wait for the foam: As the coffee heats up, a frothy foam will start to form on top. This is called "kaymak," and it's a desirable characteristic of Turkish coffee if you're not into a foamy top, just cook through a little more until the froth dissolves.

5. Pour the coffee: Once the coffee starts to foam, and just before it reaches a boiling point, pour it into the small serving cups. Fill each cup evenly while ensuring that the foam is divided among the cups

6. Serve and enjoy:

Turkish coffee is traditionally served with a glass of water, which is sipped before drinking the coffee to cleanse the palate. Allow the coffee to settle for a moment before sipping slowly and savoring the rich flavors. The Fortune-telling tradition is of course optional after drinking the coffee.

Remember, making Turkish coffee is a slow and meditative process, allowing the flavors to develop gradually. The art of making Turkish coffee lies in achieving the perfect balance between heat and time to create a delicious and aromatic coffee experience.

You can find and connect with me via email or please see my LinkTree
el@evolveology.co.uk
LINKTREE
https://linktr.ee/eljedras

Together, we can evolve
El

GRACE FULLER

Grace is an Artist, and an upcoming Co-Author, who loves to share her love of nature and its healing power of joy, happiness, love, magic, and imagination through art.

Grace is in the process of launching a healing through art course, where she will help others learn how to paint, draw, or color their emotions and feelings.

With her experiences and journey, Grace is learning just how powerful art and being creative is. A wonderful, fun, and great way to help oneself heal after trauma.

A Mother's Angel

There once was a young girl silenced by chains of words from those who were supposed to guide and love her. Annebeth spent many years a prisoner of criticism, control, and conditioning on what a young girl and woman should be. How they should act, dress, play, love, who to be around, and when to and not to talk. Annebeth began to be broken down, slowly and methodically from the age of ten. She did not start seeing the truth until she was 29 when the one who would show her that she is worth much more was born her child, her angel, her freedom from the years of abusive chains that had been placed upon her by others. This is when her eyes began to open to what really had been going on in her life.

As Annebeth held the little one against her breast, she realized that she had to do things differently. She realized that she had spent every bit of her life doing what everyone else thought she should do and what they thought was best. She knew it was going to be a long hard road to get her and her new baby to where they no longer had to fear the words and actions of others. Before Annebeth could get out of the abuse she was drowning in she would have to endure more. As she would go through the abuse, keeping her child safe, and getting themselves out, she would have to face her past, what led her to be where she was, and why she thought it was normal for her to endure all of this…

On Halloween when Annebeth was almost 7 her father took her and her brother to meet his new girlfriend, Dinna, and her son for the first time. This would be the beginning of the end of Annebeth being Annebeth to the fullest. Dinna was at their house every weekend and it was a good, busy Christmas. The following summer was similar, full of family activities and trips to the beach. Dinna even planned special girl's weekends for her and Annebeth. Annebeth was really loving Dinna being a part of their family, she didn't get to do anything like this with her real mother who was hardly ever around. Right before school started back up, Dinna stopped going home altogether. Annebeth and Tony loved having Dinna and Dylan around, they could come home from school and have someone help them with homework and play outside, without having to go to the neighbor's and just sitting inside until their dad got home from work.

The year Annebeth was in the 3rd grade her papa (Grandpa), her favorite person in the world, was moving to the mountains. She was so upset and heartbroken that she wouldn't be able to see him as often and wondered why he was moving and her grandma was staying. Annebeth got a chance to ask her papa when he asked her if she wanted to go to the mountains with him for the summer. She found out that he wanted to go to the mountains so he could keep his family farm up together and not sell it. Her grandmother wanted to stay close to family, they were not getting a divorce and her papa let her know he would be back every weekend and for birthdays and holidays.

Annebeth went back home after a summer full of hard work, fun, and meeting family from all over at her papa's to the news that she would be having a new sister. This was a huge shock, but Annebeth was so excited, she yelled "I'm going to have a real-life baby doll!" Dinna did not look happy with her excited comment. "NO, this baby is not a doll and will not be played with or treated as such." This is where things started to change. The baby was born right before Annebeth turned 10.

The summer Annebeth's sister Margaret was 2, Annebeth came back from spending time with her papa in the mountains, and Dinna, Dylan, and Margaret were not there. At first, Annebeth didn't think much of it and figured they were spending time with Dinna's family. One weekend their father came home with Margaret but not Dylan or Dinna, the next day Annebeth asked why, and her father got teary-eyed as he answered, "Because Dinna is no longer happy." A week or so before school started back Annebeth's father asked, "How would you feel if Dinna came back to live with us?" As the honest outspoken preteen, she was, Annebeth answered "I do not think it is a good idea, she left and has not tried to come back, she has made everyone sad and has hurt all of us. If she comes back, she may do the same thing." Her father was in tears, as he responded, "You are right, but we would have your sister here with us all the time." Dinna, Dylan, and Margaret all came back to live with them again.

Over the next 2 years, Annebeth started to feel as if everyone, other than her papa, didn't want her around anymore. When Annebeth had plans to spend time with her grandmother for the weekend Dinna would say to her, "Why don't you just stay here, let your brother go, your grandmother likes him better anyways and doesn't care for you to be around, we will do something special." Annebeth would tell her grandmother that she had other plans and stayed with Dinna to help around the house. A real-life Cinderella was being born. If Annebeth said anything to her father about it, Dinna always had something to say in response to undermine what Annebeth was saying or feeling.

One day when their father took them to the gas station for their weekly treat Annebeth became sad, she told her father all about the things Dinna had been saying about her grandmother and him not wanting her around and bothering them. Dinna was not around to stop her. This time she got to tell her father everything. When they got home, her father seemed like he was going to put a stop to it all, but Dinna had a clever explanation: Annebeth was taking things the wrong way because she was jealous that they were back and she no longer had her father to herself. Her father ended up agreeing with Dinna. Things like this happened for years. Annebeth started to agree that she had to be jealous, but she knew she really wasn't, but everyone was telling her she was, so she had to be.

At 18 Annebeth was back living with her father, stepmother, 8-year-old sister, and a new baby brother who was 2, after a period of living with her real mother's parents. Only things got worse, not better. Now everything Annebeth did or didn't do she got in trouble for. Her stepmom was starting to keep her out of school to help at the house with her new little brother. After missing 2 weeks of school, Annebeth went to school mad and frustrated. She was behind in all her classes and felt like she was drowning. She already had poor grades and barely passing; all the no-shows and missed assignments made everything worse. One day unaware of the assistant principal's presence Annebeth screamed as loud as she could, "FUCK THIS SHIT!!" The assistant principal heard this and was shocked that those words had come from Annebeth. She told her not to use that language again. Annebeth's response was "You don't fucking understand what is going on, none of this shit is fucking fair!" The assistant principal said, "Go to ISS, now", ISS means in-school suspension. Everyone in there was surprised by Annebeth's presence including the teacher. When the other kids went off to lunch the ISS teacher went to Annebeth with concern and asked, "What brings you in here, and what is going on?" This was honestly the first time any adult had asked Annebeth that question and showed any type of concern. Annebeth filled her in on everything, it was a very tearful lunch period. The ISS teacher decided to make it to where Annebeth had to come back each day that week to help her get caught up on her schoolwork. But she couldn't just tell her she had to come, Annebeth had to do something to get sent to ISS, so she did. When Annebeth walked into her first-period class she yelled, "Fuck" and the teacher pointed and would say "ISS NOW". All of Annebeth's missed, late and extra assignments were sent to the ISS room. Each day the teacher helped her with her work. It was the first time that any teacher or adult showed any helpful concern with her studies.

Annebeth's stepmom got a letter from the assistant principal and devised a plan to punish her. Two weeks went by and Annebeth was so excited she no longer was grounded. She came home and her father was waiting for her, with a letter in his hand. The same letter her stepmom had but only this one had been created by her stepmom. Annebeth's eyes were filling up with tears as she realized what her stepmom had done. Annebeth in pure disbelief, wiping her tears off her wet face grabbed the letter and softly said, thinking her father could not hear her, "that bitch…" Her father snatched her up and spanked her with his belt as he pulled his wife to his side. This woman had been playing her and her father this whole time.

Dinna was worse than the evil stepmother from Cinderella and her father was so deep into her spell it could not be broken. The only thing Annebeth could do was find a way to leave this hellhole. Annebeth met this very handsome young man, he was in the military and 2 years older than Annebeth. Annebeth had it in her mind, "This is my way out". The two of them became very close. The relationship became very serious very fast. Annebeth found out she was pregnant. But there was no way Annebeth was going to tell her stepmother or her father. The Army man had a plan to go ahead and get married and get base housing or a place out in town for them. When Annebth finished school, they would move in together and tell everyone they are pregnant. The end of school was only a month and a half away, this could work, Annebeth thought.

The following Friday Annebeth chose to skip school so they could get married. They had to drive almost 3 hours away to where the Army man lived but nothing went as planned. They came back to the school very late; everyone was already lined up for the awards, Annebeth's brother warned her she needed to get home as their father was pissed that she hadn't been at school all day, especially as he had been waiting for her due to the awards ceremony. With fear covering her body, she looked at the Army man with tears building up in her eyes. Annebeth knew she had to beat her father home and tell him that she was pregnant. Annebeth hoped Dinna would understand as she went through the same at her age, she had her son right after she turned 18.

Annebeth got out of the Army man's truck and walked over to her mad as a hornet stepmother, "Where in the hell have you been and why did you skip school?" Her stepmother yelled as she was standing over Annebeth. Annebeth's knees were weak and she felt sick to her stomach. "I'm pregnant" came stumbling out of Annebeth's mouth. Her stepmother snarled at the girl "You are what?" just as Annebeth's father pulls up, "he is going to be madder than me, when he hears this." Dinna starts running to Annebeth's father's car, "Your daughter has ruined her life, she has gone off and gotten herself pregnant."

Every night was lecture after lecture about how Annebeth ruined her life, and how she wasn't ready to be a parent when she was only a child herself. One night her father walked out of the room, but Dinna stayed and closed the door. She asked hatefully, "What are your plans for this kid?" Annebeth, with her tear-soaked shirt, wiped her face with her sleeve and said, "You are right, I can't raise this child, I need to do something else,". Before Annebeth could finish Dinna said "I am glad you have come to your senses, I have already set you up an appointment, you will go Friday. Army Man will take you and I will pay for it." Annebeth, confused, looked up and asked with a puzzled voice "What do you mean, an appointment to get checked out and see when the baby is due, or with the adoption place?" Dinna, with her evil stepmother laugh, said "Ha you think I'm going to let you have this baby. You will have an abortion, and you will come home and tell your father that you were never pregnant then I will be grounding you with the worst punishment you have ever had." Annebeth was truly scared. Annebeth looked at her as she was crying, putting her hands over her stomach and said with a squeak in her voice "You want me to do what? I thought I would give her up for adoption and let you and my dad raise her." Dinna said "You think I want to raise your snotty-nosed brat? You will have this abortion, or I will see to it that you lose this baby even if it lands you on your deathbed. Now call Army Man." Dinna handed her the phone and the Army Man with no hesitation agreed. Annebeth was scared for her life, and could not tell anyone what had just happened, who would believe her? The abortion took place and Army Man picked her up from school a couple of weeks later, Annebeth told him to take her home with him. They left that night, with nothing but the clothes on her back.

These moments from the past along with more played over and over in Annebeth's mind every time she looked at her new baby. She was going to prove to herself and this new baby that she was worth more than she had been dealt her whole life. She took the verbal abuse from the baby's father, the physical abuse, being thrown across the rooms, being choked, and being told that she was worthless. But she always put herself in between the child and his father. She was not going to let him put his hands on that child. She had had enough. She put herself through school, with the best grades she had ever had in her entire life, all As. She got the job that would get the ball rolling for her to support her and her child. She got a better job. She was able to get a place for them lined up. One day, the last day he would ever put his hands on her, he threatened to kill her the next time he saw her, so she went to the police. It took almost a year, but she was able to leave with her child and go back to the place she grew up, back home with her father. Now 36 years old and moving back home for the first time since she was 18. After a few months, it dawned on Annebeth, why she thought her relationships were normal, her father treated her the same. He didn't throw her, or place his hands on her, but he treated her the same way, just like her ex-stepmother had treated her all those years ago.

When she was around him, she started noticing that her son had become her father's target. Annebeth had enough and told her father he was not going to treat her son that way, not now and not ever. She was no longer going to take any of the abuse from anyone ever again, nor was she going to let her son endure that abuse from anyone. She told her son that it was time to go. In the car, he told her, "I don't like Granddad, he isn't nice to me. He makes me feel like I can't do anything right at all." Annebeth had to choke back the tears that were forming. The words of her 9-year-old rang in her ears as the memories of how she felt and how she tried to tell her father the same thing about her stepmother, all those years before filled her thoughts. She looked at her son in the mirror and said "I am glad you are telling me this, I always want you to tell me when someone makes you feel bad, no matter who that person is, even if it is me. Never be afraid to tell me anything. I will always be here to keep you safe. I won't let anyone treat you badly." They drove away, wiping the tears off their faces. As they passed wild blackberries growing on the side of the road Annebeth had a memory that made her smile. Memories of the summers she spent in the mountains with her papa.

Food Memory

Annebeth's papa would walk her around the yard of his 32-acre property and show her all the different berries growing wild, blueberries, raspberries, and blackberries. Blackberries were his favorite to pick and eat. Throughout the summer they would pick the ripe berries as he told her stories about his childhood. How he and his siblings would help their mother pick blackberries to make blackberry muffins, cakes, tarts, and ice cream. Annebeth loved listening to the stories and all the goodies they would make from blackberries.

These memories would be some that Annebeth would share with her son. She knew that she was doing the right thing, she was putting a stop to the cycle of abuse, and the abuse was going to stop. She was not going to let it into her, or her son's lives ever again. In these moments she saw that it takes only one person to stand up and try to make a difference. Today she is on a mission to help others going through or that have been through something similar find healing through art and mindset change. She knows the road to healing isn't the same for everyone and healing is a non-stop process, but she is taking the steps to help herself, her son, and others to find that healing and peace inside them.

Blackberry Cobbler

Ingredients

- 2 ½ cups fresh or frozen (thawed and drained) blackberries. (Do not use blueberries).
- 1 cup of sugar
- 1 cup of All-Purpose Flour
- 2 teaspoons baking powder
- ½ teaspoon salt
- 1 tablespoon of lemon juice (optional if you would like a tangier/tart cobbler).
- 1 tablespoon of lemon zest (optional to go with the lemon juice)
- 1 cup of milk
- ½ cup butter, melted
- Whipped Cream, Ready Whipp, or Ice-cream, if desired

Instructions

1. Preheat oven to 375 degrees F. In a medium bowl, stir together blackberries and sugar. Let stand for about 20 minutes or until fruit syrup forms.
2. In a large bowl, stir together flour, baking powder, salt, and milk. Stir in the melted butter until blended.
3. Spread batter mix into an ungreased 8-inch baking pan.
4. Spoon on the blackberry mixture over the batter.
5. Back in the oven for 45 to 55 minutes or until dough rises and is golden brown. Serve warm with Ice Cream and/or Whipped Cream topping.

Tips and Notes

Tip 1 A basic Blackberry Cobbler dough, which is like a drop biscuit, it should be mixed with a gingerly hand (easy/light) not overworked, so it will rise up through the berry mixture and have a light texture. Mix just until the dry ingredients are moistened.

Tip 2 Try adding ½ teaspoon of warm baking spice, like, Cinnamon, ginger, nutmeg, or cardamom to the dry cobbler ingredients for an aromatic edge. You can stir in a teaspoon of vanilla into the berries to enhance their natural sweetness.

Tip 3 Summer berries can take a basic cobbler beyond an everyday dessert. For a twist try adding raspberries or strawberries to the blackberries for a different flavor combination.

Tip 4 Try mixing 1 tablespoon of lemon or lime juice with 1 tablespoon of lemon or lime zest with the fruit before baking for a fresh and more tangy flavor twist. Serve warm with ice cream and or a cream topping like Cool Whipp, or Ready Whipp.

To connect with me, check out my art work, course (currently a work in progress, but soon to be active), and to see what I'm up to now check out my linktr.ee:
https://linktr.ee/GracefulArts ;
for all my social media and websites.

Love and Magic
C.Grace

Wall of Empowerment

YOU ARE INSPIRIRING

ME TOO! I HEAR YOU!

I LOVE YOUR STYLE

YOUR BODY IS YOURS

Trust your intuition and instincts.

Self-care

Be better

Women can achieve anything they want to.

Love

Positive, supportive & inspiring women groups

You made me feel important

Counselling

Journalling, Meditation, and Mindfulness

BEING SEEN AS A PERSON NOT AN OBJECT.

a tribe that vibes!

I am proud of you

"THERE IS NO LIMIT TO WHAT WE, AS WOMEN, CAN ACCOMPLISH."
– MICHELLE OBAMA

International Women's Day

YOUR STORY CHANGED MY LIFE, NOW I AM EMPOWERED

You are loved

Becoming a Mum

KINDNESS, LOVE, AND FRIENDSHIP

PROMOTED ON MERIT

"EACH TIME A WOMAN STANDS UP FOR HERSELF, WITHOUT KNOWING IT POSSIBLY, WITHOUT CLAIMING IT, SHE STANDS UP FOR ALL WOMEN."

— MAYA ANGELOU

Printed in Great Britain
by Amazon

28757046R00082